FROM PUNT
TO PLOUGH

Fen barges loaded with reed being pulled by horses in the late nineteenth century. (*CC*)

FROM PUNT
TO PLOUGH

A HISTORY OF
THE FENS

REX SLY

First published in the United Kingdom in 2003 by
Sutton Publishing Limited · Phoenix Mill
Thrupp · Stroud · Gloucestershire · GL5 2BU

Reprinted 2003 (twice), 2004, 2006

British Library Cataloguing in Publication Data
A catalogue record for this book is available from the British Library.

ISBN 0-7509-3398-4

Title page picture: Inundations have always been part of life on the Fens. These men are harvesting
corn by punt in 1912, when 10½ inches of rain fell in the months of July and August. (CC)

Typeset in 11/13.5 Sabon.
Typesetting and origination by
Sutton Publishing Limited.
Printed and bound in England by
J.H. Haynes & Co. Ltd, Sparkford.

Contents

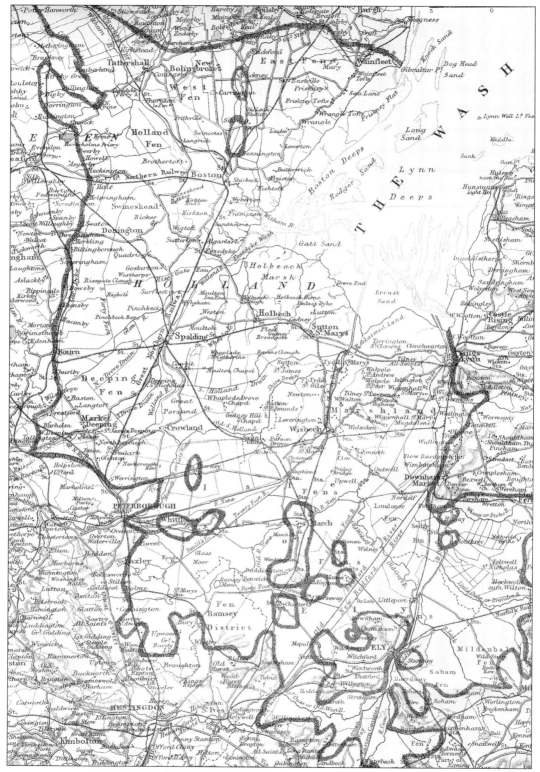

A map of the Fens dating from the late nineteenth century.

Introduction

I cannot claim that my ancestors were warriors with Hereward the Wake, the last of the Old English, nor the Normans he did battle with, who became the New English: I can, however, claim to be a true fenman. In 1273 the name Sly was recorded at Huntingdon, on the edge of the Fens, and from the mid-sixteenth century my family can be traced back to the southern and central parts of the Fens. There was a George Sly in Peterborough during the Civil War, and a Richard Sly from Dogsthorpe later in the century, and from the eighteenth century property transactions mention many Slys around Thorney.

Some of our family still live and work in these areas, doing what we have done here for three and a half centuries, farming and draining. In this sense my ancestors did fall in battle, not against their fellow men but against nature: theirs are the bones of drainers, farmers and, perhaps somewhere through the centuries, Fen Tigers. It is because of my deep roots in this area that I look back at the world my ancestors lived in and try to evaluate what has been achieved and what lost in these Fens. Every generation does what it believes to be right during its span on earth, and history tells us what we did and could have done; but it is the visionary who shapes our future and makes our history. Inevitably mistakes have been made in creating our environment, as mistakes have in many other fields and chapters of our history – foresight is too often based on the will to change without evaluating the alternative. Gone, for example, are the meres and moors, osier and reed, turburies and salterns; gone are gunners and decoys together with their quarry; gone are the millions of eels and the eelmen, who are but memories and fables to the fenmen of today. I mourn the loss of something so beautiful and untamed as the Fens one thousand years ago, but I am also aware that I did not have to eke out a living then and endure its hardships and uncertainties. Instead my ancestors have left the legacy I share today with others, a rich farming area, the feedlot for many and home to people who have come to live here. Slys are still farming in the Fens and serving on three Internal Drainage Boards across the land that our ancestors drained. There are many other families throughout the Fens who carry on this tradition, passed down from generation to generation, people whose forefathers passionately believed that the Fens needed to be drained and cultivated for themselves and their fellow men.

It is our duty to preserve what others laboured for and at the same time to remember what we owe to mother nature. I would like to dedicate this book to the adventurers and drainers of the past, for their vision, determination and unending resilience in creating our heritage. I am particularly indebted to the many men and women who today maintain the enormous task of keeping the Fens from inundation so that we can live, work and farm here – to the Environment Agency, their engineers and clerks; to the Internal Drainage Board members and Commissioners; to the people who operate and maintain the equipment to manage water for drainage and irrigation; and especially to the men who man the pumps, managing the engine room of the Fens on a constant vigil, day and night, to provide us all with a safe haven.

Rex Sly
July 2003

CHAPTER ONE

'City, Mead & Shore'

THE FENS

The counties of Lincolnshire, Cambridgeshire, Norfolk, and in a minor way Suffolk all lay claim to a part of the Fens. The Fens consist of fenland and marshland. Fenland is the land at some distance from the sea, which has been drained and protected from water from the highland rivers; marshland has been reclaimed from the sea. Since Roman times the landmass of the Fens has increased by one-third of its present-day size, thanks entirely to the ingenuity, hard work, and determination of mankind, to make up the largest plain in the British Isles, covering an area of nearly three-quarters of a million acres, which is roughly the size of the county of Surrey.

The rivers running through the Fens have a catchment area from the surrounding high country five times the size of the Fens themselves, making a total area of over 4 million acres to be drained. These rivers are all gravity fed through the Fens into the Wash and are almost all above the level of the land, some many feet higher. The fenland waters are pumped into the main drainage dykes and drains that traverse the Fens and from there they are pumped up into the rivers above or near the coast

An artist's impression of a fen before drainage. (RS)

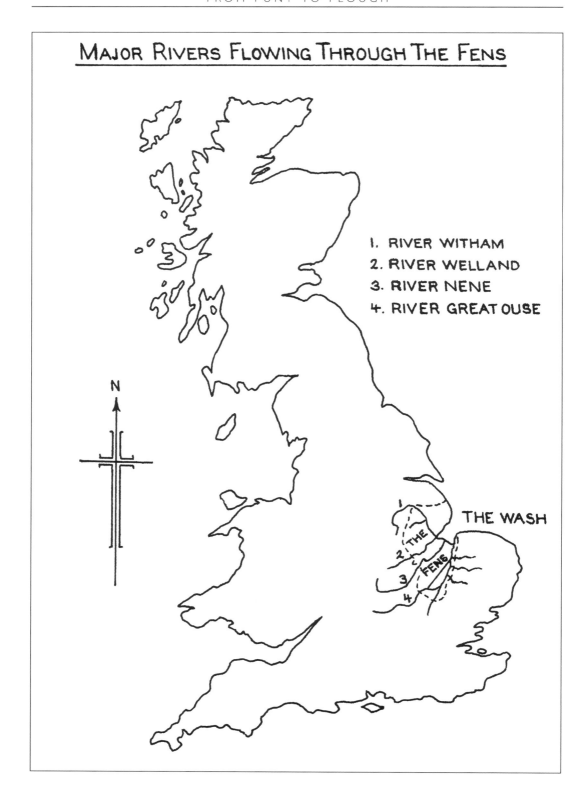

MAJOR RIVERS FLOWING THROUGH THE FENS

1. RIVER WITHAM
2. RIVER WELLAND
3. RIVER NENE
4. RIVER GREAT OUSE

THE WASH

THE FENS

directly into the Wash itself. Many low-lying areas are pumped twice and some three times before being discharged into rivers. The total pumping capacity of all the pumping stations in the Fens is capable of moving in the region of 10 million gallons of water per minute when they are all in operation. Add this to the highland water passing through the Fens and this gives one some idea of the water that is discharged into the Wash at times of flood. This highlights the management and expertise needed to maintain the status quo created by run-off. For thousands of years this has happened but what has changed is surface run-off, the time difference between the water being deposited on the soil or man-made surface and passing into the drains and rivers, a man-made problem created by urbanisation and changing farming patterns.

On his journey through the Fens Daniel Defoe (1660–1731) described this area as being 'the soak of no less than thirteen counties'. The main rivers discharging their waters through the Fens are the Witham, Glen, Welland, Nene and the Great Ouse, all beginning their life in the surrounding uplands. There are other small rivers of no less importance, such as the Little Ouse, the Steeping, the Wissey, the Lark as well as smaller becks, lodes and eaus all adding to this soak. The Great Ouse is the longest of them all, over 150 miles in length, with its source not far from the Cotswolds, gathering water from five counties on its way to the Wash. Its catchment area is over 2,600 square miles, or 1.5 million acres in total. Both the rivers Nene and Witham have catchment areas of over 1.6 million acres each from which to gather water and carry it to the Wash. The River Welland rises under Studborough Hill, 3 miles south-west of Daventry, and is joined by many tributaries on its way to the Fens, with a catchment area of over 0.45 million acres.

For thousands of years these rivers have gathered their waters from the hills and gleaned the soils of its finest particles of earth to be deposited in the fenlands. Forests blended with peat and over time decomposed, leaving us with rich black peat soils. Since the Ice Age the rise in sea levels at different periods caused large areas to be covered with seawater, and the inhospitable North Sea has also enriched this land with marine estuarine muds gathered from around our shores. These natural phenomena have left a legacy of soils unique to the Fens, silts, clays and peats of many variations. And just as it was water, from the sea and the uplands, that endowed us with this legacy of precious soils, so, ironically, it would be water that was to become man's greatest adversary in controlling them for his own exploits.

Valuable topsoil that mother nature has taken several thousand years to create can be destroyed by one man during his lifespan on earth. Nowhere is this more in evidence than in the Fens themselves. The complex drainage system we have in the Fens today has been created over a period of almost 1,500 years, and would require several volumes and maps to explain how it evolved. Indeed, many books have been written and will continue to be written on this subject, for the question of Fen drainage is a never-ending, ever-changing phenomenon fuelled by controversy.

BOG OAKS

One of the characteristic features and great wonders of this area are its bog oaks, found in the black peat soils bordering the southern edges of the Fens. The ancient forests that have left this legacy flourished from the Neolithic Age, and were made up largely of oak (80 per cent of the total), but also of elm, birch, Scots fir, yew, hazel, alder, willow and sallow. The bog oaks are now buried in the peat soils but appear on the surface occasionally like skeletons of prehistoric monsters from a bygone age, spirits from the past to remind us of what was once here. They are found mainly around Holme Fen, but have been uncovered along the northern fringes of the Fens as well, usually exposed during the course of deep cultivations or land drainage. When the ploughs catch them they are uncovered by mechanical means and carted out of the fields for disposal. Piles of oak, pine or yew of varying sizes can be seen by the roadsides or near farms where they are cut up for burning as domestic fuel, or sold as garden features. As the depth of the peat soil is

Bog oaks at Holme Fen below the surface along a fen dyke after cleaning out. The deposits of estuarine mud can be seen between layers of upland deposits illustrating the climatic changes over a period of thousands of years. (RS)

The stumps of bog oaks are sold for garden features. (RS)

This bog oak would have been over 90 feet tall. (RS)

decreasing so are the number of bog oaks; they, like the great meres, will one day be just another Fen legend, with only relics remaining in suburban garden ornaments. Some bog oaks have been recorded measuring 90 feet in length, with no branches below 70 feet and severed 3 feet above the base. Historians say that these oaks lay in a north-easterly direction and that the storm that destroyed them must have come from the south-west. The oaks in Holme Fen, however, lie in a south-westerly direction, suggesting that a violent storm from the north-east destroyed them. Most of the oaks have their stumps still on them while some have been broken off about 3 feet above the stumps, indicating that they were buried beneath peat before the storm.

The trees that can be seen today protruding from the soil on the side of the dykes lying in a layer of estuarine muds with a layer of peat above and below illustrate three distinct climatic changes that occurred over long periods of our history. The dark layers were caused by fresh water from the high land surrounding the Fens, which deposited soils that brought a regeneration of trees, plants and shrubs. This was followed by a rise in sea levels that caused flooding and layers of estuarine mud to cover the decomposed vegetation. The third change occurred when the sea levels fell, causing the uplands to flood the Fens once again with fresh water, forming new deposits of soil. These unique features can only be seen in certain parts of the Fens, mainly in the south, east and west sections or other low-lying parts, which would be the last to be drained. Today we can see them as the areas of black peat soil, or what remains of them. The variation in distance of the catchment areas of each river and the differing rainfall in those areas would only affect the parts of the Fen those rivers flowed through. This caused some parts of the Fens to flood while other parts, perhaps only 20 miles apart, remained dry, illustrating the effect these catchment areas had, and still do have, on the Fens themselves. With only natural drainage in the Fens at that time deposits of soil particles would have accumulated quickly, causing a mammoth build-up. This is evident by the post indicating the wastage of peat in Holme Fen since 1852, almost 13 feet in fifty-two years. Bog oaks have been uncovered over many years in varying depths of peat as it has shrunk and wasted, which may indicate that no one storm destroyed them but several. One tree I measured is 42 feet long, 3 feet in diameter at the base and 2 feet where it has been sawn off, making it probably 80 to 100 feet in length. It is also worth noting that the first branches were 30 feet from the base and the condition of the tree was excellent. The trees must have been hundreds of years old before they died and had ideal growing conditions to achieve this size, and, being of such mammoth proportions, must have reached maturity before the peat formed because forests and peat do not go hand in hand. We cannot be precise about the age of these trees because even carbon dating techniques cannot reveal such significant detail, but evidence suggests that we are looking at a period of many thousands of years back in our history.

HISTORY OR MYTH?

Many of the early writings and maps relating to pre-sixteenth-century drainage were in the hands of the religious houses that proliferated in the Fens during the Middle Ages, but as many of these were plundered by the Danish invaders of the ninth century or were destroyed in the Reformation much of this early information has been lost. Fire was another hazard: Crowland Abbey had one of the most extensive libraries in the land, but in 1091 was destroyed by a great fire. It is this lack of written sources that has led many historians and writers to speculate on what degree of drainage and embankment was carried out during the late Roman and medieval periods in the Fens. As H.E. Hallam says in *The New Lands of Elloe*, 'Few parts of England can have their history so grossly misrepresented as the Lincolnshire Fenland, ignorance and interest have combined to produce a hardy myth, which continues to perpetuate itself, even now, in the works of reputable authors.' In part this ignorance has been due to the absence of major trunk roads and industrial urbanisation, which has left the fen soils undisturbed, except to the fenman's plough, for hundreds if not thousands of years. This has preserved the past to some extent and kept historians and archaeologists in limbo. But we are now seeing major changes in the Fens, with mass house-building, increasing industrial expansion and a more extensive road programme, all of which could unearth many historical facts and quell the 'hardy myths'. With almost all the Fens under intensive arable farming much of the surface evidence of our past has already been destroyed. Such progress is inevitable, but for some it will lessen the mystery of the Fens and its past. For my part I pray that the origins of the dykes and sea banks, the names of villages and places may never be disproved by modern science, to spoil our dreams and fables; for without these the Fens will never be the same. A life without mystery is like a sleep without dreams, refreshing but unenchanting.

THE EARLY YEARS

To understand the intricate network of drains, rivers and bridges, together with the pumps, sluices and slackers we have today, it is essential to look back in time at man's achievements and failures. Evidence from all the major periods of human existence – from Bronze Age to Iron Age, from Romano-British to medieval – is to been seen in and around the Fens, denoting the importance of this land for settlement. At Maxey, on the north-west edge of the Fens, flint implements have been found and aerial photographs clearly show up the boundaries of a Neolithic settlement. At Flag Fen near Peterborough there is a Bronze Age settlement, discovered partly as a consequence of the construction of a new gas power station in 1982. Now one of the most important sites of this period in Europe, this was the first proof of Bronze Age human activity in the Fen, and was preserved under layers of peat in remarkable condition. In the past few years the extensive gravel extraction works between Peterborough and Thorney have revealed further evidence from this period, suggesting that agrarian practices were carried out here on a commercial scale rather than mere subsistence farming.

Wingland New Bank, 1910. Most pre-seventeenth-century drainage took the form of embanking, not drainage proper, as this photograph shows. (CC)

The Romans had several garrisons on the edge of the Fens and evidence has been found of settlements in the Fens themselves. In 2002, when the Weston bypass was being constructed, new evidence was unearthed of a Roman settlement at Weston, 2 miles east of Spalding. The coastline of the Wash recedes inland and has always been a natural receptacle for the tides. Wainfleet and Burnham in Norfolk were major Roman ports and with the many rivers running inland for long distances this must have made the Fens attractive for ships. We can assume that many of today's inland towns and villages were also used as ports or staging posts for the transport of goods. Aerial photographs have also revealed the sites of other Roman (and medieval) settlements. At certain times of the year, especially when the fen soils are void of arable cropping, these pictures are perfect platforms for this panoramic x-ray of the past.

The Romans were attracted to the Fens because of the fertile soils and their products, such as fish, eels and waterfowl, but also because of the tradition of extracting salt from the sea along the tidal stretches of the Wash, which in Roman times would have been much further inland than it is today. There is considerable evidence of Iron Age and Romano-British salterns in several parts of the Fens, and new finds are still being unearthed to further our knowledge. Much has been written on this subject, especially by Heritage Trust of Lincolnshire and the Cambridge Unit, both of which have carried out and continue to carry out extensive excavations and research in this field.

While some evidence of Roman settlement is undisputed, other evidence is open to interpretation (and has been judged myth rather than historical fact). Since almost all the Roman sites that have been identified have been covered with a layer of marine

An aerial photograph of Iron Age/Roman salterns near Holbeach St Johns. (Heritage Trust of Lincolnshire)

estuarine muds, historians and archaeologists claim that the banks commonly referred to in the Fens as Roman have long been washed away. The banks, they say, were probably built later, either during the Saxon or post-conquest periods. Despite this later dating the fen people have always called them Roman, they are on our maps as Roman and I believe will always remain so. Examples are to be found between Wainfleet and Boston and between Boston and Spalding, mostly running north/south as flood defences from the sea. We also have remains of banks running east/west between Spalding, Wisbech, Cowbit and Tydd. The northernmost of these banks would have been sea defences while the southern ones were to protect the Fen from the upland waters. These waters needed to be contained so that they could be vectored through the Fens to discharge into the Wash, keeping large parts of the land from flooding.

Many archaeologists also claim that the Cardyke, which runs from Lincoln along the edge of the Fens to Peterborough, may not be Roman either, despite the fact that the Fen people have since time immemorial referred to it as the 'Roman Cardyke' (*car* being the British word for fen). The dyke begins on the east side of the city of Peterborough near Eye and skirts along the edge of the Fen. Passing Peakirk, where it meets the River Welland, it then heads north through the Deepings clutching Kings Street, the Roman road, at Kates Bridge near Baston. From there it stretches on to Bourne, the birthplace of Hereward the Wake, and close by the site of the Cistercian abbey of Vaudey, now Grimsthorpe Castle, and, still trying to make us fenmen believe it is Roman, it hugs Mareham Lane, another Roman road. Passing the Gilbertine abbey of Sempringham it would have intercepted the causeway of Salters Way, a trade route from the many salterns to the east, around Gosberton Quadring and Helpringham. It then heads along the edge of the higher ground past Sleaford, Metheringham, Brandon and on to Lincoln, to meet up with its relation the Fosdyke (*fossa* is the Latin for canal or ditch).

The Cardykes may have served a dual purpose, one taking the upland water around the Fens into rivers for discharge into the sea and the other as a navigable transport system. It could have linked the rivers Nene, Welland, Glen and Witham, making access on these waterways to Lincoln in the north. If the Romans had used this intricate system of Cardykes and rivers, they would have been following their

A Roman bank. (RS)

The Roman Cardyke east of Peterborough, within close proximity of the Roman roads of The Fen Causeway and King Street. (RS)

tendency to move themselves and their goods on water, which required far less effort and fewer bridges – which helps to explain why there remain no bridges from the Roman era in the Fens. The Cardykes may also have been of logistical importance for the transport of goods such as salt, linking to or near Ermine Street and Long Hollow, both roads of Roman origin. Near Durobrivae, the important Roman town of Peterborough, the River Nene would flow close to the Cardyke linking up to the Fen Causeway which ran from Castor eastwards to Denver in Norfolk. The Roman road of King Street commenced here, creating a link to the north of England. Other old trade routes, probably pre-Roman, near the Cardyke, were Salters Way, from Donington to Saltersford and Marham Lane from the edge of the Fens at Threekingham north to Sleaford.

The building of the dykes and sea banks required many hundreds of men, and would have had to be built over a very short space of time because of high tides. A large labour force was not available in the Fens at this time; it has to be assumed therefore that as well as the indigenous people, soldiers and prisoners of war were used. (The use of prisoners of war to dig Fenland drains and banks would last into the nineteenth century, when thousands of French prisoners from the Napoleonic wars were used in the Thorney area. Large-scale use of hand labour was also used in the early twentieth century, even after mechanical excavators had been invented.)

THE ANGLO-SAXONS

Some historians believe that when the Romans left Britain in AD 420 the Angles and Saxons from northern Europe invaded unhindered, free to burn and plunder as they wished, and virtually destroyed all traces of ancient Britain and Roman culture. However, this image of aggressive invasion has been challenged on several counts, not least because the rise in sea levels that inundated the Fens in this period has buried or destroyed much of the evidence relating to pre-Saxon settlers. Nevertheless, there is evidence that the Anglo-Saxons settled in the Fens, where they survived on fish, wildfowl and primitive agrarian practices. Settlements were scattered and survived best on the higher ground, probably through the legacy of the Roman banks. Many of the names of present-day villages bear witness to these Old English origins. Place-names ending with 'ton' (e.g. Kirton, Sutterton, Boston) denote the island settlements established by the earliest Saxon settlers, usually prefixed with the name of the head of the community. Names ending in 'beck' (e.g. Pinchbeck) denote settlements on a small stream or beck, originating from the Old Norse *bekkr*. The suffix 'wick' (e.g. Butterwick) is derived from the Old Norse *wik*, meaning creek, whereas the prefix 'tydd' (e.g. Tydd Gote, Tydd St Giles) is from the Old Saxon *tid*, meaning tide.

CHRISTIANITY

The Fens were soon to witness another invader, a peaceful one, but one that would change it for ever. The coming of Christianity was a major chapter in fen history, a turning-point, shaping its future as a place not only of worship but of governmental power, wealth and culture. The Romans built the first sea defences but it was the clergy who would lay the foundations for draining the Fens and civilising its inhabitants. Celtic monks were the first Christians to settle in the Fens, establishing monasteries at Thorney, Peterborough, Ely, Crowland, Ramsey and a nunnery at Chatteris between the seventh century and the Norman invasion of 1066, while the Benedictine order was established here in 960. The rules of this order stipulated that monks were to act as scholars and educators, and to maintain high standards of art and music in the sacred liturgy. The Benedictines added Ramsey to the list of fenland abbeys in 969, and by the time of the Reformation Ramsey Abbey was one of the richest in the kingdom.

In the twelfth century the Cistercian order established abbeys at Swineshead, Kirkstead, Vaudey and Sawtry, and in the same century the Augustinians founded an abbey at Bourne. The Cistercians, a much stricter order than the Benedictines, had split away from the Benedictines and some would later split again to become Trappists monks, a very austere order. The Gilbertines, the only English order of nuns, canons and lay brothers, was founded by St Gilbert in 1130, establishing themselves at Sempringham Abbey near Billingborough.

ABBEYS ESTABLISHED IN AND AROUND THE FENS

THORNEY

A Benedictine abbey dedicated to the Blessed Virgin Mary, St Peter and St Benedict (later St Mary and St Botolph). Founded in 662. Burnt by Danes in 870 and 972. Dissolved in 1539 and given to John Russell, the abbey was stripped of its stone

Ely Cathedral. (RS)

which went to Trinity College and the chapel of Corpus Christi College at Cambridge. Part of the church nave was repaired in 1638, with the present transept E end added under Edward Blore in 1840 and internal alterations were made in 1888.

PETERBOROUGH

A Benedictine abbey dedicated to St Peter. Founded in 665. Burnt by Danes in 870. In 1133 construction of the abbey as we know it today began. Reconstituted as a cathedral in 1541.

ELY

Originally a Benedictine abbey for monks and nuns founded by the abbess St Etheldreda in 673. Burnt by the Danes in 870 and 988. In 1083 construction of the abbey as we know it today began, and it became a cathedral priory in 1109, its first abbot being Hervey le Breton.

CROWLAND

A Benedictine abbey dedicated to St Mary, St Bartholomew and St Guthlac. Founded in 766 by King Ethelbald. The abbey suffered many disasters, from being burnt by the Danes in 870, to a fire in 1091 and an earthquake in 1118. The abbey wes rebuilt during the thirteenth century, and massive reconstruction work was carried out in the fifteenth; but all was destroyed during the Dissolution, except for the part of the nave we see today.

CHATTERIS

A former nunnery founded by the Benedictines in 980 by Aelfwena, mother of Earl Aethelwine, who also founded Ramsey Abbey. Chatteris takes its name from Chartreuse in France. The last of nine pre-conquest nunneries in England, it was rebuilt in the twelfth century and again in 1352, when it was destroyed by fire. Very little remains.

RAMSEY

A Benedictine abbey dedicated to St Mary and St Benedict. Founded in 969, dissolved in 1539 and passed to the Cromwell family, when almost the entire abbey building and contents were removed, mostly to Cambridge.

SWINESHEAD

A Cistercian abbey dedicated to the Blessed Virgin Mary. Founded in 1135 by Robert de Gresley. King John stayed here after supposedly losing his treasures crossing the Fens. Dissolved in 1536.

BOURNE

An Augustinian abbey dedicated to St Peter. Founded in 1138 by Baldwin FitzGilbert. Dissolved in 1536.

KIRKSTEAD

A Cistercian abbey dedicated to the Blessed Virgin Mary. Founded in 1139 by Hugo Broto, Lord of Tattershall. Destroyed in 1537 after the execution of the abbot and three monks, and given to the Duke of Suffolk.

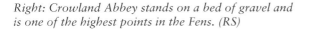

Crowland Abbey today showing the damage caused as a result of the Reformation. (RS)

Right: Crowland Abbey stands on a bed of gravel and is one of the highest points in the Fens. (RS)

Denny Abbey and Farm Museum. (RS)

Kirkstead Abbey remains after the Reformation. (RS)

REVESBY

Daughter house of Rievaulx. Founded in 1143 by William de Romara, Earl of Lincoln. Dissolved in 1538 and given to the Duke of Suffolk.

SAWTRY

A Cistercian Abbey dedicated to the Blessed Virgin Mary. Founded in 1147 by Simon Earl of Northampton. Dissolved in 1536.

VAUDEY

A Cistercian abbey founded in 1147 at Castle Bytham by William le Gros, Count of Albemarle. Dissolved in 1536. It would have stood in the grounds of what is now Grimsthorpe Castle.

DENNY

Originally a Benedictine priory founded in 1159, dependent on Ely. Transferred in 1170 to the Knights Templar but suppressed in 1308. It was re-established as a Franciscan nunnery (Poor Clares) in 1342 to replace nearby Waterbeach. Dissolved in 1539 and granted to Edward Elrington.

WATERBEACH

Founded in 1293 by Denise Munchensey, and gradually transferred to Denny because of flooding. One of only four medieval houses of Poor Clares in England. Dissolved in 1531.

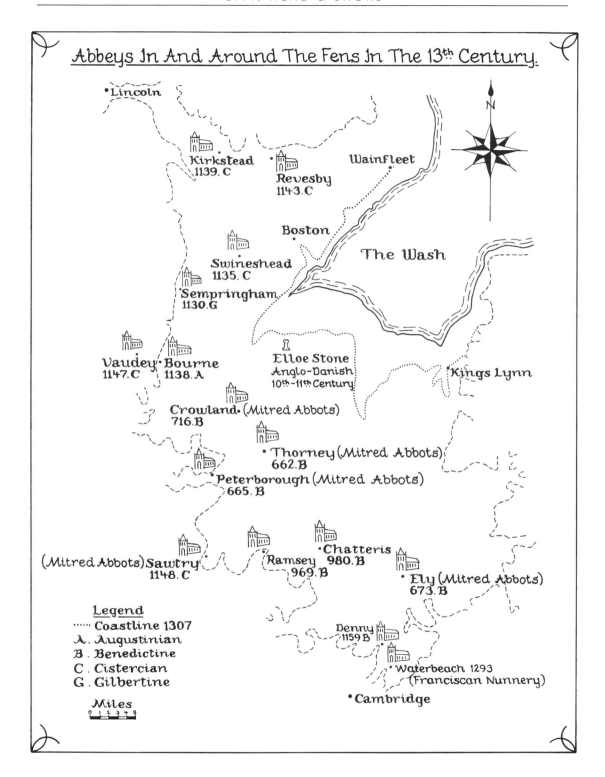

Abbeys In And Around The Fens In The 13th Century.

•Lincoln

Kirkstead
1139. C

•Revesby
1143. C

•Wainfleet

N

Boston

The Wash

Swineshead
1135. C

•Sempringham
1130. G

Vaudey Bourne
1147. C 1138. A

Elloe Stone
Anglo-Danish
10th–11th Century

•Kings Lynn

Crowland• (Mitred Abbots)
716. B

• Thorney (Mitred Abbots)
662. B

•Peterborough (Mitred Abbots)
665. B

Chatteris
980. B

(Mitred Abbots) Sawtry
1148. C

Ramsey
969. B

• Ely (Mitred Abbots)
673. B

Legend
······ Coastline 1307
A. Augustinian
B. Benedictine
C. Cistercian
G. Gilbertine

Miles
0 1 2 3 4 5

Denny
1159 B

•Waterbeach 1293
(Franciscan Nunnery)

•Cambridge

The abbeys of Crowland, Thorney, Swineshead and Chatteris were built on relatively high ground well inland, on small islands of gravel or clay surrounded by meres and low-lying peat areas, which made them very isolated. The remaining abbeys were also constructed on high ground or on the edge of the Fens: there were none in the central Fens or along the western edge. The religious settlers had come from the north and so perhaps did not wish to venture across this morass to establish their religious houses; or perhaps that part of the Fens held a hostile race of people: we will never know.

Much of the land surrounding and close to these abbeys was not drained for years to come. Thorney Abbey, for example, would wait for almost a thousand years before the Protestant refugees from Europe, the Huguenots, Walloons and Flemings, settled around its precincts and began draining the surrounding land. It would then take another 200 years for the Duke of Bedford to transform the village and its surrounding farmland into a fenland utopia, so much so that many of the families that came with the drainers of the seventeenth century are still there to this day.

BEFORE THE CONQUEST

There must have been around two centuries of peace and tranquillity in the Fens between the advent of Christianity and the arrival of the Danes. Man could survive in this land that provided for all his earthly and spiritual needs. Small-scale drainage around the abbeys took place to improve agrarian practices, leaving the rest of the Fens untouched, and man taking only what he needed to survive. The Danes however had heard of this fertile land and wanted to savour its spoils. Historians have referred to three periods of incursion by the Danes, the first between 793 and 867, in which the invaders sought simply to plunder, not wanting to settle here, but to take their spoils home with them; the second, between 867 and 1013, was a period of partial settlement; and the third, after 1013, represented political conquest and the establishment of the Danelaw. The abbeys of Thorney, Crowland and Peterborough and Ely were plundered and burnt in 870 by invading Danes, indicating that the marauders had not settled here then. We are also told that the abbey of Ely was once again burnt and plundered in 988, but that later, in 991, money was paid to the Danes by the abbot to prevent his attacking the abbey – proving that in even in those days cash was king. The suggestion of tribute would also indicate that by then the Danes were at least on negotiating terms with the abbots and had perhaps already settled in the northern parts of the Fens, possibly on the silt islands surrounding the Wash. By 1013 the Danes had settled in and around the Fens under the first Danish king, Canute, and established the Danelaw. They had either murdered or married the Anglo-Saxon people, exchanged their gods, Thor and Odin, for Christ, and lived under the Danelaw. In this kingdom, which stretched from Wessex in the south-west, through Mercia in central England to Northumbria in the north, vast sums of tribute, or Danegelt, were raised, part of which was used to buy off fresh invaders from northern Europe. Many villages and towns in these areas still have names of Danish origin: the suffixes 'by' (Digby,

Asgarby, Haconby, Reevesby and Spilsby), 'kirk' and 'toft' are found in the northern section of the Fens (Burtoft, Wigtoft and Fishtoft). In *The New Fens of Elloe* H.E. Hallam gives a good description of early Danish settlement in the Fens: 'Holland being divided into Wapentakes not Hundreds is evidence of the Danish influence in that period, not Anglo-Saxon.'

Another indication of Danish settlements can be found in the suffix 'gate' around the Spalding to Sutton Bridge area, 'gate' being the Nordic word for street or road. Other words, too, provide keys to fenland history. Wapentake is derived from the old Norse words for weapon and take – the term probably refers to the Scandinavian custom of brandishing weapons in an assembly as a gesture of assent. It is claimed that the Elloe Stone, which stands between Moulton and Whaplode, is of Anglo-Saxon origin dating between the tenth and eleventh centuries and was such a meeting place of the men of the hundred of Elloe. When the stone was re-erected in 1911 an inscription was found on the base, reading 'The Elloe Stone, erected in Anglo-Saxon times to indicate the place of meeting of the hundred of Elloe courts'. W. Stukeley further recorded, 'Old men tell us, here was kept in ancient times an annual court, I suppose a convention, *sub dio*, of the adjacent parts, to treat of general affairs.' A wood hard by is called Elhostone Wood.

The Danes, however, like the Anglo-Saxons, did little to improve the drainage of the Fens, relying instead on wild-fowling, fishing and primitive agriculture, especially since the abbeys had gone into decline. In fact they soon discovered that this inhospitable countryside was to their advantage: by leaving the Fens undrained they were provided with every necessity they required to live their own secluded lives while still keeping out intruders: it was to them a safe haven.

The Elloe Stone, near Weston, a meeting place at the time of the Danelaw.

The eleventh century saw another upheaval in the Fens, the arrival of the Norman invaders. The loyalty of the people was divided, with some staying loyal to the Old English while some would befriend the Norman invaders. The son of Leofric, Earl of Mercia and the Lady Godiva, Hereward was probably the last of the earls of Mercia. Born at Bourne in Lincolnshire, in his youth Hereward was somewhat boisterous, over-zealous and eager for adventure. His behaviour with a steward from Peterborough Abbey over money he was supposed to have taken, coupled with contempt for some of the clergy, led to his being outlawed by the king.

Hereward the Wake clearing Bourne of the Frenchmen.

He spent several years travelling abroad seeking his fortune and fighting for any cause he passionately believed in. While in France, at St Omer, he met his future wife Torfrida, who would become a legend herself in fighting battles against the Normans in the Fens. The war against King William would last for seven years with many battles fought in the marshes around Ely. Hereward was finally killed during a clandestine raid in the Fens, near Crowland. The focus for anti-Norman feeling centred around the figure of Hereward the Wake, who retreated to the fastness of the Fens after conducting raids against the Norman upstarts. Those who complied with the newcomers would also incur Hereward's wrath: when Peterborough Abbey installed a Norman abbot it paid the penalty – Hereward allowed invaders from northern Europe to plunder the abbey to avenge this outrage, while steering them along the river within one mile of the loyal abbey of Crowland.

Richard of Rulos, when speaking to Torfrida, wife of Hereward the Wake, concerning a tomb for her husband said,

'And what shall we write thereon? 'What but that which is already there? 'Here lies the last of the English.'
Torfrida replied, 'Not so. We will write, "Here lies the last of the old English." But upon thy tomb, when thy time comes, the monks of Crowland shall write, "Here lies the first of the new English; who, by inspiration of God, began to drain the Fens."'

By the time of the death of Hereward the Wake the last remnants of Old English resistance had been subdued and the Normans became firmly established in the Fens. Meres and stagnant watercourses were to be replaced by dykes and ditches to drain this fertile land, and never again would it be a refuge for guerrilla warfare.

THE CONQUEST AND AFTER

After the Norman Conquest the fenland abbeys grew in size and population, establishing manors, priories and granges in the surrounding areas as well as cells for monks to live in and spread their faith into the remote fen regions. In order to sustain themselves the abbeys introduced sheep, horses and cattle from France and were eager to exploit the Fens for agrarian purposes. The Fens would become primary producers of wool, and trading links with the continent grew up for this commodity during the twelfth and thirteenth centuries. Many of the fine churches and abbeys of the Fens are said to be built from the profits of wool traded to Flemish merchants for weaving. The ports of Boston, Fossdyke, Wisbech, King's Lynn and to a minor extent Spalding and Bicker Haven were all active in the wool trade. Peterborough Cathedral has the largest thirteenth-century painted wooden ceiling in the world and during recent restoration work on it leading dendrologists discovered that the pine planks it is painted on were of German origin from the thirteenth century – it was at this time that the Hanseatic League, an association of Northern German trading towns, was formed to protect their economic interests overseas. There was friction between the League and England

The Hanseatic League warehouse was in King's Lynn. Built in 1475, it is now in a residential street. (RS)

but trade flourished nevertheless through the Fenland ports, with warehouses in Boston and King's Lynn owned by Hanseatic merchants.

The Normans established religious houses on a much grander scale than their Anglo-Saxon predecessors. Norman abbots undertook large-scale construction works in rebuilding the abbeys, which could not have been built here were it not for the availability of suitable stone on the edge of the Fens: its soils may yield deposits of sand, gravel and ancient timbers, but not stone. Barnack had some of the finest stone for building in the country, easy to quarry, good to work with and not difficult to transport throughout the Fens. Ely, one of the great abbeys to be built in the eleventh century, agreed to render 40,000 eels a year during Lent to the abbey of Peterborough in return for building stone from Barnack. Stone was also obtainable at nearby Castor and Helpston, with slate for roofing at Collyweston. Barnack stone would be used for most of the great abbeys in the Fens and became a lucrative asset to Peterborough Abbey, which owned the quarry. Collyweston, Barnack and Helpston are all within close proximity of the River Welland, and Castor, virtually on the banks of the River Nene, made the logistics of transport into the Fens from the surrounding uplands easy, and the many hundreds of watercourses across the Fens allowed these cargoes of stone, timber and other building materials to be easily shipped to ports on the coast or to any destination required.

It is interesting to note, and still a mystery to some, that so many abbeys were built in and on the edge of the Fens. The architects who built the fenland abbeys were certainly highly skilled – I believe that none were flooded either then or later.

Several of these abbeys stand today towering above our fenland landscape, their bells echoing across the land. Crowland Abbey is especially renowned for its bells: the first peal of bells in England was rung here in AD 975, and here also the 'danger bell' tolls in time of crisis – the last time it tolled was when floodwaters lapped the abbey graveyard walls on 21 March 1947, the year nature claimed back much of her fen for a brief period.

The construction of the abbeys required skilled craftsmen, stonemasons, carpenters, roofers and an army of labourers to work for them. It is fair to assume that much if not all the labour used in these works would have been migrant labour from beyond the Fens, since up to this time the fenman had lived a simple existence requiring nothing that was not already in his immediate environment. His skills in hunting, fowling and fishing, however, were now required to feed the newcomers, and since many of these had come from Europe their culinary tastes differed from his own and necessitated a change in his farming husbandry. New crops such as flax and colza were therefore introduced. Flax was used to make linen for garments and colza seed was crushed to provide oil – as is oilseed rape is today, a major crop for farmers in Britain.

There were other innovations to the fenman's way of life in this period. Previously he only needed to catch enough wildfowl to sustain himself and his family and supply the nearby abbeys. The decoy and the plover nets had not been introduced from the continent at this time and with the Fens teeming with birds his methods of trapping made little difference to the numbers involved. The method of driving duck, wigeon, teal and other wildfowl into nets during their moulting period when they could not fly became a common practice to fulfil the demand for food and feathers. There are stories that up to 4,000 birds were taken in one drive in Deeping Fen. Commercialism had truly eked its way into the Fens.

The abbeys and the newly established Norman families owned large tracts of the Fens, while the remaining land, which was prone to inundation, was classed as common land. The abbeys retained their ownership until the Reformation in the sixteenth century, and some Norman families such as the De Ramseys and Fitzwilliams retained their rights up to the present day. The indigenous fen people farmed the common land but their rights began to be eroded in the fifteenth century when the Fens were first drained and the marsh reclaimed from the sea. In the early enclosures tenants were unable to safeguard their traditional grazing rights, which led to many people's livelihoods being destroyed. Records from Peterborough Abbey reveal that in 1300–1 the abbey farmed some 4,906 acres, which was four times the area estimated in 1125. Cattle and pig herds had doubled over that period and the number of horses and sheep increased threefold. Much of this land lay outside the fen, but we must assume that the demand for land for agrarian development was increasing in the fen itself.

During the thirteenth and fourteenth centuries the fen grew wetter and it is a fact that fen vegetation is as sensitive as woodland to human management. The abbeys' records fail to evaluate either fen or meadow resources but they do list labour services. These show that peasants mowed reed and sedges on a two- to four-year rotation and carried the cuttings to Peterborough Abbey precincts, for use as material for thatching and furniture. Some of the renders listed in the Domesday Book survey (1086–1125) also hint at the use of other resources, such as water birds. The abbey also enjoyed the products of fish and eels from the fen rivers and meres. The abbot had a boat on Whittlesey Mere and had sub-let another boat, a fishery, and fishermen from Thorney Abbey in exchange for wood and pigs from the upland behind Peterborough. The value put on these fisheries in the fen is evident in the Domesday survey, which shows a fen fishery belonging to Peterborough Abbey valued at eight shillings, a value that exceeded any one of its mills, markets, or woodlands. Processed grain in the form of fine flour, for bread, baked loaves, flour of second grade, malted grain for drink, and oat fodder constituted 34 per cent of the annual food renders of the abbey. Peterborough Abbey enjoyed a return from its estates in excess of approximately 53 per cent over its own annual consumption. In the twelfth century each fenland abbey needed to harvest between 1,000 to 2,000 acres of grain to sustain itself and to sell 50 per cent of the flour products, proving that large-scale farming is nothing new in the Fens.

First Major Drainage Works

After the Norman invasion England experienced almost four decades of relative peace and stability, and over that period the increase in population led to a demand for more food and to eliminate shortages in years of famine. The practice of managing land for rotational crops, ensuring good husbandry, was unknown in this period, and land outside the Fens had become unproductive because of the absence or the rudimentary nature of husbandry skills. But the rise in sea levels had abated, leaving large deposits of estuarine mud which, when overlaid with deposits from the fresh water from the uplands, was the making of rich the fen soils we have today.

Britain's colonies across the globe had yet to be discovered, and in 1453 England was finally expelled from its European colony, thus ending the Hundred Years War with France. And so the Fens were looked upon as a new source of food. This would be the new colony, which would require draining, protection from the tides and the management of the rivers by embanking. The only method of pumping water at this time was by the Archimedes screw, which had been introduced into Britain during the Roman occupation, although it was not capable of moving large volumes of water.

There are no accurate records of the population in the Middle Ages for England, and the figures we do have can be misleading. However, based on Domesday data and projections, an estimate would be 2.8 million in 1200, rising to 5 million in 1300, with only 3 per cent of the population living in towns. Interestingly, the population in Roman times was also estimated to be 5 million. The bubonic plague in the fourteenth century had dramatically reduced the population, sometimes causing whole villages to be depopulated. The next two centuries saw a population growth and a concomitant increase in the demand for food, all of which fuelled the need to drain low-lying areas in this country, especially the Fens.

It would be a clergyman who had the first vision of a major drainage scheme in the Fens. In the fifteenth century John Morton, Bishop of Ely, was the first person to realise that if you cut a drain in a straight line water travels faster, and brings about the scouring effect which keeps the drain from silting up. The drain he cut was 12 miles long, 40 feet wide and 4 feet deep and ran from Stanground, Peterborough, to Guyhirne. This drain steered the water from the Nene at Stanground via Guyhirne to Wisbech and then into the Wash. The previous course ran via Benwick, Floods Ferry, March Outwell and Wisbech, which was a long, slow, meandering course for the water to travel along.

The leam, the medieval name given to a drainage channel, was completed in 1480, having made use of prisoners of war from the Hundred Years War, a practice that would continue for the next 300 years. This principle of draining would eventually be the basis of all drainage in the Fens, emulated up to this day. It was as far as we know the first time in our history that man instead of nature had changed the course of a major fen river. Morton had laid the foundations for Sir Cornelius Vermuyden, who cut the drain for the second time on the same line in 1640 during his draining of the Great Level. In 1486 John Morton was made Archbishop of Canterbury and nine months later Lord Chancellor, under Henry VII. In Whittlesey an inn close by the Leam is named after the anecdote 'Morton's Fork': while Lord Chancellor Morton claimed that a sign of affluence was that you had money and

Archbishop Morton's Leam was cut in 1480 when he was Bishop of Ely. (RS)

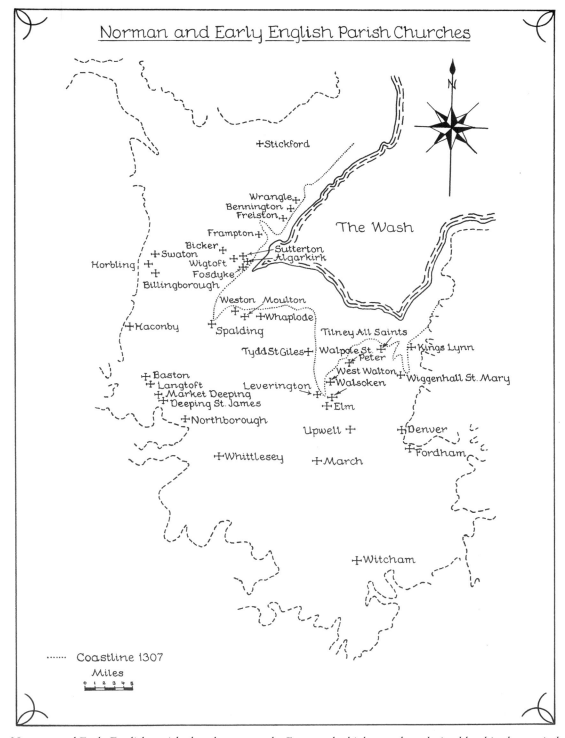

Norman and Early English Parish Churches

The Wash

+ Stickford

Wrangle +
Bennington +
Freiston +

Frampton +

Bicker +
+ Swaton
Horbling + Wigtoft +
+ Fosdyke
Billingborough

Sutterton
Algarkirk

Weston Moulton
+ + Whaplode
+ Haconby + Spalding

Tilney All Saints
Tydd St Giles + Walpole St. +
Peter +
+ King's Lynn
West Walton +
+ Baston Leverington → + Walsoken + Wiggenhall St. Mary
+ Langtoft +
+ Market Deeping + Elm
+ Deeping St. James
+ Northborough
Upwell + + Denver
+ Fordham
+ Whittlesey + March

+ Witcham

······ Coastline 1307

Miles
0 1 2 3 4 5

Norman and Early English parish churches across the Fens on the highest or best drained land in that period.

31

Algakirk church dates back to the Saxon period (RS)

The Chapel of Ease at Guyhirne was built in 1660 and is still consecrated and used for burials. (RS)

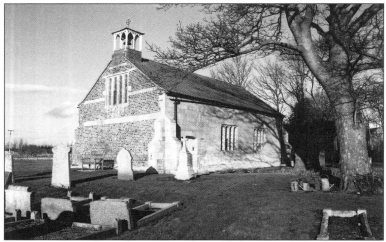

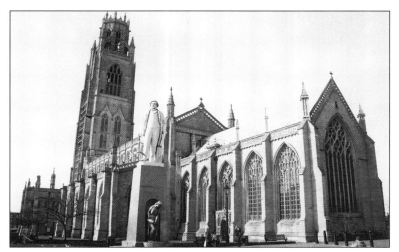

St Botolph's Church, Boston, was built in 1309 and was known as the Stump. The statue in the foreground is of Herbert Ingram MP, a Bostonian who founded the Illustrated London News in 1842 and was instrumental in bringing piped running water to the town, which many fen communities lacked. (RS)

could afford to pay taxes, while a sign of poverty was that you had hoarded money and could also afford to pay taxes. Morton's Leam remains to this day exactly where it was cut in the fifteenth century very close to the inn. It runs through Whittlesey Wash, which Vermuyden constructed in the seventeenth century as a flood plain, and is still used for the grazing of livestock and as a bird reserve.

The fenland scene would not be the same without its many beautiful churches, the earliest of which were built on islands of silt or gravel to ensure protection against floods. These churches were the cultural, spiritual and trading links that enabled people to traverse this inhospitable country safely and to survive. With more of the Fen and marsh being developed for agricultural needs the population to service this industry grew and with it their spiritual needs. Much of the area was in the interior of the Fens and on the edge of the marsh away from the great abbeys. Many of the abbeys already had cells and priories in those areas where churches were built, but churches also grew up on many of the earlier Saxon settlements.

The earliest fenland parish churches at Algakirk and Sutterton were built in the twelfth century, while almost forty were built during the thirteenth and fourteenth centuries, the remaining in the following century. Few if any areas of the country can boast this number of churches so close together and so beautiful – it is almost impossible not to see at least one if not several at a time from any vantage point in the Fens when visibility will allow. The large number of parish churches – well over 120 parish churches across the Fens built in the Middle Ages – gives some idea of the density of population here at this period, and also of the poor state of roads and bridges, which made travelling to church difficult. In 1425 the parish of Crowland alone covered some 12,780 acres and had a population of 1,801, equating to 0.14 people per acre; in 1831 its population was only 2,268, equating to 0.17 people per acre. By way of comparison, it is worth noting that in 1831 the county of Lincolnshire had 0.02 people per acre and Crowland 0.17 people per acre, representing over eight times that of the rest of the county.

SALTERNS

Before leaving this period in fen history we must evaluate the importance of salt production in and around the Fens up to the sixteenth century. Over the past fifty years dedicated historians, archaeologists, and enthusiasts have enlightened us on this very important part of our fenland history. There are two types of sites, one on marshland, where strange-looking mounds are visible, the other on fenland, where no mounds are visible. Of the former, large earth mounds can still be seen in the northern part of the Fens, notably at Fistoft, Wrangle, Freiston and further south around Gosberton, Surfleet and Quadring. There are also mounds at Fleet Whaplode, Pinchbeck and Holbeach Bank. They are found mostly along the mouth of tidal estuaries near old sea defences and on areas of silt soils. There were early theories as to their origin: some said they were built as observation posts, manned by soldiers of the Roman army to prevent ancient Britons destroying the sea defences. Another theory was that they were built by the Anglo-Saxons as

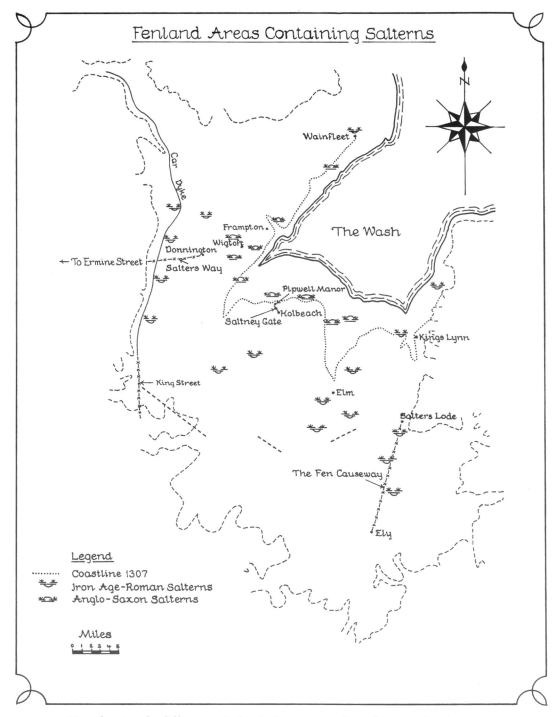

Fenland Areas Containing Salterns

Wainfleet

Car Dyke

Frampton

Wigtoft

The Wash

Donnington

← To Ermine Street

Salters Way

Pipwell Manor

Saltney Gate

Holbeach

Kings Lynn

King Street

Elm

Salters Lode

The Fen Causeway

Ely

Legend

.... Coastline 1307

Iron Age-Roman Salterns

Anglo-Saxon Salterns

Miles
0 1 2 3 4 5

Map showing the different periods of salt extraction from the sea and early routes.

observation posts where fires could be lit to warn people against Danish invaders. Many have been levelled or dug up over the centuries, but no traces of bones or other remains have been found, thus disproving another theory that they may have been places of worship or ancient burial grounds. We now know these mounds were in fact salterns, where salt was extracted from the sea.

There is firm evidence that salt was extracted in the Fens from the Iron Age up to the fourteenth century. In 1562 there was a declaration that 'much salt is made in England as of sand and salt water in pits in Hollande in Lincolnshire'. Before rock salt was discovered in 1670 the production of salt was obtained by evaporating salt water obtained from the sea. Large quantities of 'bay salt' were thus manufactured on the coasts of the Fens and on the margin of Bicker Haven, there being no less than twenty salt pans in that parish. The shallow pits by the side of the main road between Sutterton and Boston are generally supposed to be the remains of salt pits, which were supplied with water from Bicker Haven. In the Domesday Book there is mention of over 100 salt pans existing in the fenland parishes, the value of a salt pan being between 8*d* and 1 shilling. The method of procuring salt was by allowing the water brought up by the tides to run into shallow ponds, in the same manner as is still practised on the coast of Spain. The salt water was run through three pits. In the first it was allowed to remain until the mud and sand had settled, then allowed to flow into the second until it became brine. It was then run into the third pit

An artist's impression of medieval salt extraction carried out outside the sea defence banks. (RS)

Large mounds near Surfleet formed by deposits of silt from salt extraction during medieval times. (RS)

where it remained exposed to the sun until the water had evaporated and the crystals of salt were formed. This method changed during the first millennium and would be used until the end of salt extraction in the Fens in the seventeenth century. It consisted of collecting loads of silt from the shoreline, then transporting it to a site to be filtered and boiled. The deposits of silt after extraction would then be piled up in mounds which can still be seen today. Salt was a precious commodity used in the preparation of fish, fowl and meat, and the only way of preserving food. It was also an essential element in the tanning of skins and hides required for garments, footwear, armour and bags for carrying tools and weapons. Many abbeys and priories drew their rents in salt payable to their cellarer. The Crowland Abbey account rolls mention salt beds at Whaplode, Gedney and Dunton Hall near Tydd. The salt was sold by a measure, apparently of 9 bushels, which was used for salting meat in the abbey larder. Many other abbeys and monasteries in and around the Fens owned or leased land either in or outside the sea banks for salt production. Curious measures were mentioned, too: at Terrington in Norfolk there were important salt-works paying rent to Ely in bledes, wayes and gates of salt. Sometimes the pans got damaged; just before 1200 William de Roumara was granting to St Mary and the canons of Dereham the right of digging with four spades in his East Marsh belonging to Bolingbroke, for the repair of their salt-pans. Around 1180 Richard son of Jocelin of Fleet gave Castle Acre Priory 5 acres in his *cultura* of Westneueeland.

A terrier* of the village of Fleet dated about 1316 provides an example of this activity. Fleet, like its neighbours, was protected by a bank from flooding by the sea. Outside this bank lay wide stretches of silt and sand, overflowed in part by the

---

* A terrier is a register or roll of a landed estate.

36

tide. To the regular arable holdings of *workland* and *moleland* [ploughed land] within the sea wall, there were appurtenant holdings outside the wall called *hoga et area* [pasture and ploughed land] for which a rent of salt was paid. In addition to this regular *redditus assisus* [payment], a bondman, whenever he boiled salt outside the vill, paid a toll to the lord of one measure called *overgongmiddas* [full measure]. If he boiled within the vill he paid only one-half measure every *patella* [salt pan, usually of lead]. The lord also claimed a toll on all salt sold; from twenty measures when sold and carried *extra portum* [out of the lord's domain], he received one penny. Moreover, all bushels of salt from Fleet itself and from the adjoining villages of Gedney and Holbeach were brought once a year to a holy place outside the sea wall, called 'le mothow'; there, the bushels received the lord's sign as evidence that they contained true measure. Those that brought bad measure were in *misericordia* [at the Lord's mercy].

This example of Fleet may be taken as a type of the salt-making activity that went on along the silt zone throughout the Middle Ages, and continued for some time later. A recent study of three sites at Helpringham, Holbeach St Johns and Bicker Haven reveals further details, covering a period of 1,500 years or more, from the Iron Age to the Romano-British and medieval periods (*Lincolnshire Excavations at Helpringham, Holbeach St Johns and Bicker Haven*, The Heritage Trust of Lincolnshire, 1999). Helpringham on the western edge of the Fen close to the old Roman Cardyke is the site of Iron Age salterns. Even with its proximity to the Cardyke evidence suggests that salt was extracted here before the Romans came to this area. Hearths were uncovered indicating that brine was boiled to extract salt from seawater, which at that time would have come up the Bicker Haven. This site was also near Salters Way, only a few miles to the south. It is hard to believe that salt water once came here since the site is now 15 miles from the sea. The sites at Holbeach St Johns are further inland and on flat ground, not a mound like the other salterns in the Fens.

The third site is at Bicker Haven, now inland but until the seventeenth century an important port. Here are found numerous sites, probably the largest concentration of salterns in the Fens from the Romano-British and medieval periods. Excavations on these sites have shown evidence of filtration, storage and hearths for boiling brine. During the reign of Edward III (1327–77) there was a dispute between the abbots of Peterborough and Swineshead over land outside the sea wall at Bicker Haven, involving lengthy law suits at Lincoln and London. This land being outside the sea wall would more than likely have involved salterns, and at that time the abbot of Peterborough owned fourteen salt pans close to Donington, a most valuable asset to the abbey.

The salt industry, controlled largely by the great fenland abbeys, made the Fens a valuable area to control up to the fifteenth and sixteenth centuries. Place names still exist to remind us of this industry: one such name is Salters Lode between Nordelph and Downham Market, which was a navigable waterway – today it carries leisure craft rather than salt barges. In its day salt would have been shipped between North Norfolk and the religious houses at Wisbech, Chatteris, March and Ely along this tidal watercourse. Nearby at Nordelph was the Roman road, the Fen Causeway, leading out of the Fens to Ely and thence to other roads linking Roman towns in this part of England. There existed an ancient road known as Salters Way, later called Holland Road, between Grantham and what was Bridge End Priory just on the edge of the Fens north-east of Billingborough. This linked up to the treacherous Bridge End causeway across the Fen to Donington where there are numerous salterns around Bicker Haven, Donington and Quadring, where salt was produced. This land route linked up to the Roman road of Ermine Street near Grantham as well as passing close to the Roman Cardyke.

It was probably when rock salt was discovered in the second half of the seventeenth century that the laborious method of extracting salt from the sea ceased in the Fens. The Toll Book of the Dog and Doublet Sluice near Thorney on the River Nene administered by the Duke of Bedford's estate in 1731 has several tolls paid for the transport of salt up the river. Between 20 November 1731 and 29 April 1732 thirteen and a half tons of salt passed through the sluice. It is not known where it came from or in which direction it was travelling along the river. There was no salt recorded passing through the sluice between the months of May and October. It would more than likely have been used to cure hams or bacon

Turves being stacked for drying in the late nineteenth century. (CC)

Turves being dried and transported across a fen drain by wheelbarrow. (CC)

which would have been killed in the winter months. This salt could have come from far afield but it is not beyond the realms of possibility that it could also have come from salt workings still operating in the Fens themselves.

TURBARIES

Hand in hand with the salterns went turbaries, which provided fuel to evaporate the brine. *The Red Book of Thorney* (Cambridge University Library) records a grant of a *salina* in Hirneflet with right of digging turves '*extra Hassocdic ad sustenationem praedicte saline sufficientem*'. The custom of taking turbary sufficient for the fuel of a salt pan was apparently a well recognised one; and it would seem that certain portions of the turbaries were specially reserved to supply associated salt pans. In the north-east corner of the fenland, pans were important not only in Wainfleet, but also in Wrangle and Friskney. During the late fifteenth century turves were being constantly carried to these places. I live at Turfpits Farm, which is mentioned in Dugdale's book of 1620. Nearby was the site of Goll Grange belonging to Spalding Priory to which this farm would have belonged, and there is

Digging turves. (CC)

evidence of salterns close to this site in Cowbit Wash. An aerial photograph shows signs of what looks like peat diggings on the farm. Recently while carrying out test bores for a new road, remains of a saltern were found near where the Grange once stood, so it is fair to assume that this farm was used to dig turf for boiling brine from the saltern.

CHAPTER TWO

'Brethren of the Water'

THE FEN CODE

For hundreds of years the Fens were a unique area of Great Britain, not only in terms of ecology but also in terms of its people and their way of life, with certain elements remaining unchanged until the nineteenth century. Since the reign of Edward VI in the sixteenth century a code of fen laws had been enacted to define the rights and privileges of the commoners, and to prevent disputes and robbery. The Fen Code of 1549 was drawn up by the Council of the Duchy of Lancaster at the Great Inquest of the Soke of Bolingbroke, held in 1548, and was confirmed in 1573 during the reign of Elizabeth I. The code remained in force until the enclosure of the Fens at the beginning of the nineteenth century. It consisted of seventy-two articles, a short summary of which may be interesting as affording an insight into a state of society now passed away for ever.

One of the first rules of the code related to the brands or marks which each person who stocked the Fens was required to place upon his cattle. Each parish had a separate mark and no man was allowed to turn cattle out to common until they were marked with the town brand.

Swans and other waterfowl being fed during winter on Welney Wash. (RS)

No foreigner, or person not having common right, was allowed to put cattle on the Fens, under a penalty of forty shillings; fish or fowl at any time; or gather any turbary or fodder in the Fens, without a licence from the approver, under a penalty . . . for each offence.

Penalties were also attached to the following: putting diseased cattle on the Fens; disturbing the cattle by baiting with savage dogs; leaving any dead animal unburied for more than three days; putting swine on the Fens, unrung, or geese which were not pinioned and foot-marked; taking or leaving dogs there after sunset; bringing up crane birds out of the Fens. Rams were not allowed to be kept in the Fens between St Luke's day (18 October) and Lammas (medieval harvest feast held on 1 August). No person was allowed to gather wool who was above twelve years of age, except impotent persons; no cattle were to be driven out of the Fens, except between sunrise and sunset; and no cattle were to be driven out of the Fens during divine service upon the sabbath, or holy days; all cattle were to be 'roided' or 'voided' out of the Fens before St Barnaby's day, yearly; no reed thatch, reed star, or bolt was to be mown before it was of two years' growth; each sheaf of thatch gathered or bound up was to be a yard in compass; wythes were only to be cut between Michaelmas and May-day; no man was allowed to 'rate' any hemp or flax in the common sewers or drains. Every township in the parts of Holland, claiming common in the fen, was ordered to show to Queen Elizabeth's steward, at the next court-day, its charter to common right. No swans', cranes' or bitterns' eggs , or any eggs excepting those of ducks and geese, were allowed to be brought out of the Fens. No fodder was to be mown in the Fens before midsummer day annually. No person was allowed to use any sort of net or other engine, to take or kill any fowl, commonly called moulted ducks, in any of the Fens, before midsummer, day annually.

Rooding by hand is still done when machines are unable to operate, usually around urban areas.

A code of seventeen articles was also devised by the fishermen's jury, in relation to the fish and fishing in the Fens. The principal fish referred to were pike, eels, roach and perch. The laws related to the kind of nets allowed and to the manner of using them.

A Fen drover's card. (Spalding Gentlemen's Society)

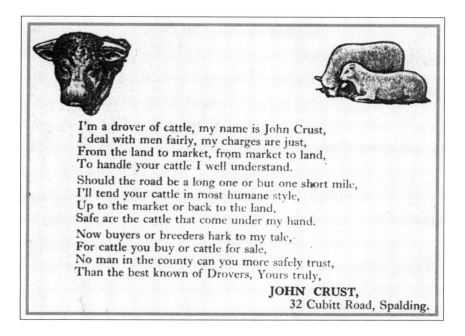

I'm a drover of cattle, my name is John Crust,
I deal with men fairly, my charges are just,
From the land to market, from market to land,
To handle your cattle I well understand.

Should the road be a long one or but one short mile,
I'll tend your cattle in most humane style,
Up to the market or back to the land,
Safe are the cattle that come under my hand.

Now buyers or breeders hark to my tale,
For cattle you buy or cattle for sale,
No man in the county can you more safely trust,
Than the best known of Drovers, Yours truly,

JOHN CRUST,
32 Cubitt Road, Spalding.

Before being sent into the common fen, the livestock were collected at certain defined places and marked, and again, on being taken off in the autumn, they were brought to the same place to be claimed by their owners.

Thus at Pinchbeck the stock were collected at the market cross and a due called hoven was paid. Bailiffs were appointed to look after the stock. On the marshes in South Holland a marsh reeve and a marsh shepherd were appointed annually, their wages being paid by a rate of 1s 6d for each horse and neat beast, and 3d for each sheep, grazed on the commons.

The Fens remained in the condition described until the year 1762, when an Act was obtained for the improvement of the low lands on the Witham, with the river being straightened and deepened and the Grand Sluice at Boston erected.

CHANGES IN THE AIR

Between the eleventh and fifteenth centuries land ownership in the Fens was concentrated mainly in the hands of the great abbeys and Norman families. Abbeys as far afield as York owned land here, a not uncommon situation in this period, when many abbeys owned land at great distances from their diocese. Domesday Book, for example, shows Crowland Abbey owning some fifty parishes over six counties of England.

Major changes in land ownership came about at the beginning of the fifteenth century, however, when at the close of the Hundred Years War with France land in England that had previously belonged to French abbeys was confiscated and given to many newly founded colleges and hospitals. This legacy still holds today, and there are still many farms in the Fens belonging to Cambridge and Oxford colleges. Further, and even more dramatic changes came about as a result of the Dissolution of the monasteries between 1536 and 1539, when not only was land given to the new colleges, but stone was recycled to build more colleges and chapels (as well as houses in the Fens). Some abbeys in the Fens were demolished completely, such as Sawtry, Sempringham, Bourne and Ramsey, leaving very little evidence of their existence, while others such as Crowland and Thorney were reduced in size.

The Dissolution was also to reduce the power of the abbots in parliament. After the Norman Conquest the wealthier abbeys had 'mitred abbots' who paid taxes to help fund expenses for the public needs. In 1370 every mitred abbot paid as much tax as an earl and 6s 8d for every monk in his monastery. There were twenty-five 'mitred abbots' in parliament until the mid-sixteenth century, five of whom came from the Fens – from Ely, Ramsey, Thorney, Crowland and Peterborough. Lincoln, although not in the Fens but overlooking parts of the northern Fens, also had a 'mitred abbot'.

These changes in land ownership presented many problems locally. As Tudor courtiers were rewarded for their favours with large tracts of fenland, the changes rippled out to much smaller owners as well, leading to administrative problems that made it difficult to coordinate repairs to banks and drains. Widespread flooding in the Fens occurred frequently and the state of the Fens deteriorated gradually over the years until counter-measures were taken in the early part of the seventeenth century. Absentee landlords, living hundreds of miles away, had no intention of setting up their residences in the Fens, unlike the great fenland abbots who came to worship God and reside here. After the Dissolution it was no longer the Holy Land of England; for the next three decades it would become 'the land of Adventurers'.

EARLY LEGISLATION AND SCHEMES

The demand for food to sustain the expanding population of the country and to avoid periods of famine during poor harvests was essential to maintain stability. Fen drainage therefore began to attract the attention of monarchs and their ministers; the need to establish some form of legislation to supervise and coordinate schemes was vital if the land was to become a primary producer. In 1258 Henry III appointed one of his ministers, Henry de Bath, to draw up a commission 'to look into the inundations of the sea in parts of Holland, Lincolnshire'. This was followed by another commission in 1266 'to enquire by jury of the parts of Holland' the names of those responsible for repairs; and to distrain all those who had lands in the Wapentake of Elloe in Hoyland to make walls, dykes, bridge and sewers. This was the first of many such commissions over the next 250 years that would lay the foundations for the future drainage of the Fens.

The commissions appointed juries to decide which landowners were responsible for waterways and banks against inroads of the sea. They could also enforce repairs and were empowered to levy taxes and fines from defaulters if they thought fit, and, provided they observed the law, their acts were not examinable by any court of law. The commissions originally had a life span of only ten years which, although later extended to twenty-five years, meant that the improvements to the drainage system lacked continuity and long-term planning. Before the Dissolution, the Commission of Sewers lacked any real powers and the abbeys and riparian landowners carried out such drainage as they felt necessary. There was at times very little cooperation between them and even conflict where responsibilities for the maintenance of dykes and flood banks were involved. In between new commissions being set up delays occurred for long periods and disputes often took years to settle.

This situation was improved slightly in 1531, when the General Sewers Act was passed, giving the commissions more powers but still not enough authority to carry out drainage schemes. However, when Henry VIII passed the famous Statute of Sewers in 1532, which limited his own prerogative powers by granting more scope to the various commissions, there was still not enough coordination and cooperation between the parties involved. The overlapping authorities of different kinds had drainage powers and were ever jealous to keep them, often vying against each other. This state of affairs was to remain the basis of drainage legislation until the nineteenth century and as such kept this country lagging behind our continental neighbours; indeed, disputes over drainage and flooding would continue into the twentieth century.

The seventeenth century was a period of intense draining and embanking in the Fens with the aim of combating flooding from the sea and the uplands. The mid-sixteenth century saw attempts to drain parts of the Fens by cutting straight drains not seen since Morton's Leam in the 1480s. The Maud Foster drain and the Hobhole drains were cut in 1568 and 1569 to improve the drainage of the east and west Fens north of Boston. Efforts were also made in the southern Fens to eliminate flooding problems in 1605 when an Act of Parliament was passed. The Lord Chief Justice under James I, Sir John Popham, left his mark at this time with Popham's Eau, a straight drain carrying water from Three Holes to Nordelph. This medieval eau would have carried salt from Salters Lode up the old salt route to join the Fen Causeway that Hereward the Wake made famous. Thomas Lovell in 1603 proposed draining land near Bourne and Deeping Fen, but his ambitions were larger than his finances and so these Fens remained undrained.

Until this period embanking was the main method used in the prevention of flooding, but in 1603 many embankments burst after heavy rain, causing severe flooding in the Fens, and destroying farms, homesteads and villages. There was an enormous loss of life to people and farm animals throughout the Fen regions, which caused the king much grief. He knew there had been widespread neglect in maintaining embankments and drains since the Dissolution of the monasteries. When informed of this calamity, the king declared that, for the honour of his kingdom, he would no longer suffer these countries to be abandoned to the will of the waters, nor let them lie waste, and he himself would become the 'undertaker'.

Acts of Parliament relating to drainage in the reign of James I, together with appointed commissioners of sewers, paved the way for the visionaries of the day; indeed, it could be said that James I was the first true drainage adventurer in England.

The area he was concerned with first of all was the low-lying land north of Boston, the east and west Fens, lying between the sea and the higher ground of the Lincolnshire Wolds. The logistical problem here as in many parts of the Fens was a ridge of high silt land along the Wash, which the floodwater could not pass through to discharge into the Wash and so would have to discharge into the Witham outfall. The main stumbling block, however, was the lack of finance. Parliament would not agree to fund it and so the plan was not undertaken.

Undaunted by the lack of funds to carry out these two schemes, the king persisted in his passion to drain the Fens and turned his attention to draining the Great Level in the south of the Fens. This area consisted of a much larger area of fen than the east and west Fens; it was further from the Wash but had many of the same logistical problems for draining. It would prove to be the most ambitious project ever undertaken by any engineer in the land, if not in the world, up to that period in history.

THE VISIONARIES

Continental practices in land drainage were beginning to influence Englishmen at this time. In particular, Holland had been a source of inspiration. Protestants who had been persecuted in France and Belgium had been welcomed to Britain during the reign of Elizabeth I, as they were during the reigns of James I and Charles I. Huguenots from France and Walloons and Flemings from Belgium had escaped Catholic persecution to settle in the Fens, especially around Thorney and Whittlesey, and many families of Huguenot and Walloon descent still live and farm in the area to this day. These people were much in demand by the drainers here, having first-hand experience in this field as well as being agriculturists in their own right. They not only had drainage experience but also brought new crops and agrarian practices in cultivation and land management. Many had also been involved in the draining of the isle of Axholme, so had learnt the ways of the English and their hostility to foreigners.

King James I himself had used the Dutch engineer Cornelius Vermuyden to drain land at Windsor and also to repair banks on the Thames and Canvey Island. Plans had already been submitted to the king to drain the Cambridgeshire Fens, but as he died in 1625 he never saw his dream fulfilled. His successor, Charles I, shared his passion and in 1626 instructed Vermuyden to drain Hatfield Chase in the isle of Axholme situated in the north of Lincolnshire. Hatfield Chase was not a complete success but Vermuyden had made his name in land drainage in 1630 under what was known as the 'Lynn Law', a scheme initially devised by Charles I to drain the Great Level. The king, however, like his father, was unable to raise funds from parliament to finance the scheme – one of many conflicts with parliament that would eventually culminate in the English Civil War (1642–51).

Sir Cornelius Vermuyden, knighted in 1629 for his drainage work on the Thames, Hatfield Chase and Axholme for James I. He later drained large areas of the Fens.

Right: Francis Russell, 4th Earl of Bedford. (By kind permission of the Marquess of Tavistock and the Trustees of the Bedford Estate)

Fortunately, the 4th Earl of Bedford came to the rescue as principal undertaker; together with other adventurers they backed the venture for a sum in excess of £100,000. The greater part of this was financed by the Earl himself, and it is believed that he also underwrote many of the other adventurers' investments. For the Bedfords this was the beginning of a family tradition of drainage in the Fens that would continue for the next 300 years, in fact until the last of the family estate was sold off in the 1930s. The fen people living in the area called the Great Level, but especially those in the North Level, are indebted to this family more than to any other in history associated with this land, for they were truly great adventurers. The Bedford connection with the Fens goes back many years. Sir John Russell, (1486–1555), 1st Earl of Bedford, Lord Privy Seal in the reign of Henry VIII and Edward VI, owned a considerable estate at Thorney. The estate was enlarged when the family was granted extensive property by Henry VIII after the Dissolution, not only in the Fens but also in Bedfordshire, Devon, Cornwall and London.

William Russell, created Baron Russell of Thornhaugh (situated near Wansford) by James I, was also the owner of thousands of acres around Thorney. He was the youngest son of the 2nd Earl of Bedford and while Governor of Flushing in Holland had seen the Dutch building dykes and reclaiming land from the sea. These activities impressed him immensely and he brought three Dutch engineers over to look into the feasibility of continuing drainage work in the Fens. He was granted permission by the Privy Council to carry out various schemes. When William died in 1611 his son Francis, 2nd Baron Russell of Thornhaugh (1588–1641), became, on the death of his cousin Edward in 1627, 4th Earl of Bedford. He laid the foundations for the draining of the Great Level, or the Bedford Level as it would be known, but it was the 5th Earl, William Russell (1613–1700), 1st Duke of Bedford, who went on to create the Thorney Estate. A unique man who lived under five sovereigns and Cromwell's Protectorate, he was also responsible for the formation of the Bedford Corporation in 1663 to drain the Bedford Level, which was to last 257 years until it was dissolved in 1920 after a most turbulent existence. Thus the Russells were the pioneers of Fen drainage, and would remain so until the nineteenth century, which, together with their knowledge of the lands they owned and their desire for constant improvement in the techniques for new farming methods, made them leaders in this field.

The area drained by the 4th Earl William Russell covered approximately 100,000 acres of the Fens, mainly around the Earl's estates of Thorney and Whittlesey, but also included land stretching from Ely in the south to Bourne in the north. Much of this consisted of low-lying land many miles from the river outfalls, with the water having to pass through areas of higher silt before it entered the Wash. There would be many unforeseen problems in the project that would test the minds of engineers for generations to come. The works were to be overseen by Sir Robert Heath and two Dutch engineers, Sir Philibert Vernatti and Cornelius Vermuyden, with Lord Edward Gorges the Director of Works. The largest of the drains cut (since Mortons Leam back in 1480) was the Bedford River (later Old Bedford River), some 70 feet wide, running from Salters Lode to Earith, a distance of 21 miles. It is hard to imagine the logistics of such an operation undertaken without machinery – the workforce must have been huge.

Other major drains either cut or improved on this scheme:

Bevill's Leam, from Whittlesey Mere to Guyhirne, 2 miles long, named after Sir Robert Bevill

Sam's Cut, from Feltwell to the Great Ouse, probably named after adventurer William Sames, doctor of common and civil law

Morton's Leam, improved, from Peterborough to Guyhirne, cut in 1480

Sandall's Cut, near Ely

The Peakirk drain, which took high country water through the Fen from Peterborough Fen to Guyhirne

New South Eau, from Crowland to Clough's Cross, a medieval drain that brought water from Crowland, winding its way through Dowsdale, Throckenholt to Clough's Cross, which would have been tidal then. At Clough's Cross the South Eau ran into the Shire Drain which was also improved past Gannock Grange, (once owned by Spalding Priory) where it is known as Lady Nunns Old Eau and on to the Sluice at Tydd Gote

The outlet from **Tydd Gote** to the sea

Cloughs are sluice gates that allow fresh water to flow in one direction, thus stopping the sea flowing the other way. Most of the cloughs today, Holbeach, Ravens, Clough's Cross and Gosberton are many miles from the sea.

Many of the early drainage works were not a success and so some ten years after the Lynn Law (1630) Charles I asked Vermuyden to draw up a *Discourse on Draining the Fens*. In the southern section of the Fens he proposed to drain 170,000 acres of which Francis Russell, 4th Earl of Bedford, and his joint undertakers were to receive 58,000 acres, rising to 95,000 acres on completion. This left many of the local inhabitants bitterly opposed to the scheme because they gained little of the drained land and in fact would face poorer livings. Vermuyden's report to the king on the draining of the great Fens, the particulars of which are fully set out in his *Discourse on Draining*, published in 1642, advised that the rivers Glen and Welland should be diverted to the Nene, and the waters of the three rivers carried in one common outfall to the sea. Andrew Burrell opposed this

Horseway Locks on Vermuyden's Drain, cut in the seventeenth century. This drain runs into the Old Bedford River, also cut in the same century at Welches dam. (RS)

scheme in a pamphlet published in 1642. It is interesting to note that almost 200 years later, in 1839, Sir John Rennie proposed a scheme to join the rivers Witham, Welland and Nene and the Great Ouse together as one, with one outfall into the Wash.

Vermuyden succeeded in shortening the course of the Great Ouse by about 10 miles, but the river would prove a major problem for years to come. This second phase of Vermuyden's work entailed the New Bedford River to be cut parallel to the old one with the flood washes in between known as the Hundred Foot Washes, or, as many of us know them, the Welney Washes. At the same time he created Whittlesey Washes as a flood area for the River Nene and Crowland and Cowbit Washes for the River Welland. These are Vermuyden's trademarks, and I believe will remain so for as long as the Fens are populated by people who wish to farm and live here.

There were many problems for the drainers at this period in the Fens apart from the logistics of the schemes. Apart from Vermuyden's unpopularity, which in itself caused discontent, the introduction by foreigners – largely Protestant refugees who had settled in the area from 1606 onwards – of new farming techniques and crops to the Fens brought jealousy and ill-feeling. It must also be remembered that during this second phase of draining the Great Level the English Civil War was being waged, and was especially fierce in the Fens. While, during the Protectorate, prisoners of war (from Cromwell's campaigns in Scotland and Ireland, and from the Battle of Dunbar in 1650) were marched down to the Fens for hard labour Cromwell incited the fenmen against the new schemes by openly stating that Charles I, by draining the Fens 'was feigned to serve his country and its people and his sole interest was his own pocket'. These words were manna to those fenmen whose ancestors some 500 years earlier had rallied to arms against a foreign tyrant – to such men, who saw their precious fen being destroyed by outsiders and foreigners, Cromwell was the reincarnation of Hereward the Wake.

With all these opportunities for dispute, the activities of the drainers could not but provoke disorder. Their newly erected dykes were destroyed; their channels were filled in; their sluices were kept open at flood tide and closed during ebb. Restlessness was abroad throughout the entire region, and rioting was frequent in many parts of the Fens. As early as 1606 fensmen were saying, 'they need not the help of foreign undertakers', while those who supported the schemes in 1629 were saying, 'Is the old Activities and abilities of the English Nation (who in former times were esteemed the greatest undertakers in the Westerne parts of the world) growne so dull and insufficient that we must pray in aide of our Neighbours to improve our own Demaynes?'

And again:

For matter of security; shall we esteem it a small moment to put into the hands of Strangers three or four such Ports and Harbours as Lynne, Wisbech, Spalding, and Boston. . . . and permit the Countrey within and between them to be peopled by over-thwat Neighbours whose strength and undertakings begin to grow formidable. . . . What, indeed is Cole-Seed and Rape, they are but Dutch commodities and but trash and trumpery.

To express this dissatisfaction 'libellous songs to disparage the work' were composed and circulated through the region, such as 'Powte's Complaint'. Here are five of the ten stanzas:

POWTE'S COMPLAINT

Come, Brethren of the water, and let us all assemble,
To treat upon this matter, which makes us quake and tremble;
For we shall rue it, if 't be true, that Fens be undertaken,
And where we feed in Fen and Reed, they'll feed both Beef and Bacon.

They'll sow both beans and oats, where never man yet thought it,
Where men did row in boats, ere undertakers bought it:
But, Ceres, thou, behold us now, let wild oats be their venture,
Oh let the frogs and miry bogs destroy where they do enter.

Behold the great design, which they do now determine,
Will make our bodies pine, a prey to crows and vermine:
For they do mean all Fens to drain, and waters overmaster,
All will be dry, and we must die, 'cause Essex calves want pasture.

Away with boats and rudder, farewell both boots and skatches,
No need of one nor th'other, men now make better matches;
Stilt-makers all and tanners, shall complain of this disaster,
For they will make each muddy lake for Essex calves a pasture.

The feather'd fowls have wings, to fly to other nations;
But we have no such things, to help our transportations;
We must give place (oh grievous case) to horned beasts and cattle,
Except that we can all agree to drive them out by battle.

Adventurers involved in the early drainage works in the Fens in 1630 were:
Francis Russell 4th Earl of Bedford, Baron Russell de Thornhaugh
Oliver, Duke of Bullingbroke
Baron de John deBletsow
Henry Lord Maltrevers
Edward, Baron Gorges
Robert Heath, Chief Justice of the Common Court of Pleas
Miles Sandys of Wilberton, Knight Baron
William Russel of Chippenham, Knight Baron of the King's Ships
Robert Bevill of Chesterton, Knight of the Order of the Bath
Thomas Tyrringham of Terringham, Knight Baron of the Order of the Bed Chamber
Robert Lovet of Licombe, Knight

Philibert Vernatti, Knight of the Order of the Kings Bed Chamber
Cornelius Vermuyden, Knight
William Sames, Doctor of Common and Civil Law
Antony Hammond of St Albans of the Order of Armour Bearers
Oliver of St John of the Order of Armour Beaters
Samual Spalding
Andrew Borrowell
John from Haesdonck

The drainage works carried out in the Fens during this period were the largest ever undertaken in this country and nothing would compare to them for the next 200 years. So successful was Sir Cornelius Vermuyden's work that in 1652 'the Bedford Level was declared drained', and a thanksgiving service held at Ely Cathedral. Mother nature, however, had other ideas!

The Fens had been being transformed into the richest farming land in the country, a new colony of England with many rich speculators eager to share in its riches, but not to live there. There are no stately houses here – some would say the setting is not enchanting – and some of the finest abbeys in the land were destroyed by the very people who wished to own a part of this land. In a similar vein we have the same thing today, with hardly any of the owners of tenanted land residing in the Fens themselves: is it any wonder the fenmen have always been wary of outsiders and foreigners even to this day?

Curiously, the history of the Fens may have taken a different course if Charles I's fortunes had proved less trying. While Vermuyden was cutting the Bedford Rivers Charles came to the Fens and watched operations from a piece of high ground near Manea. So much did he love the surrounding countryside that he proposed to build his summer residence here and name it 'Charlemont'. Work was started on the palace but did not progress because of the Civil War and his execution. But Charles's vision is exemplified by the work of John Fellows, the Lord de Ramsey of Abbots Ripton, who lives on the edge of the Fens and whose family is of long standing in this area. Actively involved in farming like his ancestors before him, as well as being a landlord of many fenland acres, his knowledge as an agriculturist and the subject of fen drainage is second to none, and as a custodian of the countryside he is a shining example to all fenland landowners.

The seventeenth century witnessed many other adventurers in the Fens in that period, one of which carried out work that James I had envisaged, in the north and east Fens north of Boston.

The first major scheme in what is now known as the Black Sluice was begun in 1635–8, known as the Lindsey Level, lying in the north-west part of the Fens. It was undertaken by the then Earl of Lindsey and other adventurers, who were contracted to the Lincolnshire Commissioners of Sewers to carry out a main drainage scheme for the reclamation of 36,000 acres. This area, like much of the Great Level, was low lying, subject to constant flooding and some distance from the outfall into the Wash.

Although the scheme resulted in the building of the first recorded sluice (probably known as Skirbeck Sluice, very close to the present site of the Black Sluice), like many of its kind in this period it was not a great success, and much of these Fens would be subjected to flooding for the next 200 years. The legacy of this scheme, however, was the South Forty Foot Drain, which became the nucleus for the drainage of this area in future years and still is to this day.

In 1720 the Earl Fitzwilliam, another adventurer, had estates at North Kyme on the edge of the Fens. The water from this area had to pass down the River Witham to discharge at Boston. With a view to relieve the winding river he cut the North Forty Foot drain which now serves as the main drain to Cooks Lock pumping station and Holland Fen pumping station and at the same time constructed a sluice at Lodewick's Gowt. The drain was originally known as Earl Fitzwilliam's drain, aptly named after this adventurer, but at some time in our past was changed to the North Forty Foot, another loss to our fenland history.

THE MARSH

Not only was land being drained and reclaimed in the Fens but adventurers were also reclaiming land from the sea. There was a vein of silt stretching from Wainfleet to Boston then across to Spalding and from there it appeared as small islands hopping across to Sutton Bridge and on to King's Lynn. This was formed from silt being washed from the sea enclosing the Inner Fens where Romans, Anglo-Saxons and Danes had settled and constructed banks as sea defences. Many of the villages

A sketch of early reclamation from the marsh. (RS)

on these silts bear names of Danish and Anglo-Saxon origin. This area also boasts some of the finest examples of parish churches you will find in the land, and exemplify the fenland landscape.

It was the churches established on this causeway in the twelfth and fourteenth centuries and settlements around them that began the task of reclaiming marsh from the sea. There were then many small tidal rivers, such as the Moulton, Whaplode, and Holbeach rivers, the Fleet Haven, South Eau and the Lutton Leam and what is now the South Holland Drain that crossed the area. From this causeway across the Fens the fenmen would push back the sea, an enormous challenge that required completely different techniques from those used in reclaiming land from the Fen. With two tides a day haste in building the banks was vital, as was the use of a large labour force during the short periods the tide was out. High tides and lashing gales coming down from the North Sea would test the sea banks to the extreme. During times of flood, water from the surrounding high country would also test the sea defences, causing more havoc than the sea. But the fenmen's resilience won the day, establishing a foothold across the Fens. By undertaking reclamation on two fronts the fenman was to extend his kingdom over the next five centuries.

ENCLOSURES

The enclosing of common land had been increasing since the fifteenth century throughout the whole country, but in the Fens enclosure meant drainage or embanking to keep the tides out. For example, the old tidal rivers of Whaplode, Moulton and Holbeach and Fleet as well as Gosberton, Bicker and other smaller rivers winding their way into the Fens were banked and sluices built at their outfalls. This invariably caused hardship to many of the fen folk in these areas and it was not until the General Enclosures Acts of 1836–45 that tenants' rights were safeguarded.

The enclosure of common land had been gathering momentum throughout the country since the fifteenth century, but in the Fens the pace accelerated in the seventeenth century, particularly in the marsh areas, where the salt industry was in decline. Salterns were brought inside the sea walls, and many thousands of acres were enclosed and converted to farmland.

One of the earliest records of enclosures is that of a grant made by James I to C. Glemmond and John Walcot of London, as nominees of the Earl of Argyle, of certain salt marshes in Wigtoft, Moulton, Whaplode, Holbeach and Tydd St Mary, which were to be drained at the expense of the Earl. One fifth was to be reserved for the king, and also certain common lands of the neighbouring townships. Others granted land 'inned' or banked from the sea in the same period were the Earl of Carlisle, the Earl of Lindsey, Sir Peregrine Bertie and Sir Philip Lunden. Sutton and Lutton marshes, covering 6,700 acres, were enclosed in 1660, as were 1,600 acres around Bicker Haven, 1,632 at Tydd St Mary and a further 17,374 acres were enclosed by certain adventurers in the parishes of Gedney, Holbeach, Whaplode and Moulton.

The General Drainage Act of 1663 had permitted enclosures even on non-corporation land, causing disputes and unrest in this part of the Fens, so much so that the Enclosure Prevention Act of 1684 repealed the right to make further enclosures in the Bedford Level. Fenland enclosure was somewhat different, however, from the enclosure of common land that took place in other parts of the country, where the open-field system prevailed. In the Fens, both fen and marsh were mainly given over to grazing and the land was subject to frequent flooding: enclosure here therefore meant drainage or embanking to keep the tides out which, in the long term, brought ecological change. For example, the old tidal rivers of Whaplode, Moulton, Holbeach and Fleet, as well as Gosberton, Bicker and other smaller rivers that wound their way into the Fens, were banked and sluices built at their outfalls. This invariably caused hardship to many of the fen folk, and even the loss of their ancient hunting grounds, their source of fish and wildfowl. Sadly, throughout the whole of the enclosure movement little regard was given to the peoples whose lives were directly affected by the changes to their natural environment, until the safeguards afforded by the General Enclosures Acts of 1836–45.

Enclosures continued in the Fens during the late eighteenth and early nineteenth centuries, when thousands more acres were enclosed and drained to stimulate food production. One of the largest enclosures in this period was at Deeping Fen and Crowland in 1801, when 15,000 acres were enclosed. But even up to the early twentieth century thousands of acres were still being embanked by hand labour in the marsh; which made the 'managed retreat' of 1992 all the more ironical, and difficult to bear.

Where ducks by scores travers'd the Fens,
Coots, didappers, rails, waterhens;
Combin'd with eggs, to change our pot,
Two furlongs circle the spot;
Fowl, fish, all kinds, the table grac'd
All caught within the self same space;
As time revolved, in season fed,
The surplus found us salt and bread;
Your humble servant, now your penman,
Liv'd thus a simple, full-bred Fenman.
                    *William Hall**

Fen slodgers.

Shrinkage

When the mammoth drainage schemes of the seventeenth and early eighteenth centuries were completed and began to take effect on the Fens, an unforeseen consequence set in, the emergence of aerobic bacteria, which lowered the surface of the peat. The more fen peat is drained, the more it contracts, and shrinkage, as it

* The author lived on a small island near Kyme Fen and at that time was the last person to have been born on the island.

The author standing next to the post at Holme Fen showing the shrinkage of peat since 1852. (RS)

Right: Wicken Fen, the only remaining wind engine driving a scoopwheel. (RS)

The remains of a scoopwheel in Holland Fen, probably dating from the early twentieth century. (RS)

Tongue End showing the level of the land on the right well below the river on the left. A pumphouse can be seen on the opposite bank of the River Glen which pumps water from Bourne Fen up into the river. (RS)

would be known, occurs: a phenomenon the Dutch engineers had not experienced in Holland and which would become a major problem over the next 300 years. Gravity discharge alone could not move water off the Fens, and with many of the rivers now above the land (because of soil shrinkage) water would have to be lifted into them. This required pumps of some description to lift the water into the drains and dykes. The first ones used were scoopwheels driven by wind power, or wind engines, as they were called, the idea coming from Holland. Hundreds were erected all over the Fens to pump water up into the drains; the problem was they only worked when the wind was blowing. Hayward's *Survey of the Fens* of 1635–6 mentions an Ingin and an Ingin bank at Oxney Farm, which was mentioned again in the St Ives Court of Sewers in 1638. At Connington in 1644 there was an engine 'for the keeping of the grounds dry'. Daniel Defoe, in his *Tour through the whole of Great Britain* in 1724 mentioned 'some wonderful engines for throwing up water', and one in particular threw up 1,200 tons of water in half an hour.

Drainage in the Fens, however, made little progress until the invention of the steam engine and the centrifugal pump. Before the invention of the steam engine it was said there were over 700 wind pumps working throughout the Fens, while in 1852 there were still over 150 in use and the scoopwheel itself was used even after the invention of Applod's centrifugal pump in 1852. Wheeler states in 1896 that there were still a few around. The only remaining wind-powered scoopwheel is at Wicken Fen Nature Reserve, managed by English Nature, and the remaining steam-powered ones are at Pinchbeck and Stretham.

The never-ending urge to master the management of water for agrarian purposes would bring other unforeseen consequences, changing the Fens for ever, socially, economically and ecologically. For some an exciting new world had been created, but for others the changes brought destruction to a way of life never to be experienced again, and a new breed of fenmen. One can sympathise with the indigenous fen people resisting the adventurers and foreigners. Many lost their

A willow yard where willows were stripped and then delivered to the basket makers, mainly by boat, around the end of the nineteenth century. (CC)

Rosewell Pits, Ely, 1895. Gault had been dug here for three centuries. In the foreground is a wildfowler drying his nets. These would have been used to net plovers. (CC)

smallholdings through massive drainage schemes where the adventurers, in return for draining the Fen, were given land. The enclosures of common land also deprived the small farmers of their livelihood. Drainage often meant the destruction of meres for fishing and fowling, reed and sedge being replaced by cropping. For many the Fen had everything that man needed to live on, eels and fish, fowl and fruit, as well as pockets of soil as rich as any on earth. The rich fertile soil nurtured his grain for beer and bread, provided rich pasture to fatten cattle and sheep and still left grazing for horses. Osiers, sedge and willow grew in abundance for him to use as he wished and salt, essential for life, was available from the sea, extracted in salterns, for preserving food and tanning hides. Poppies enhanced his garden and endowed him with opium to relieve the ague, his penance for living in the Fens.

VERMUYDEN'S WASHES

Vermuyden foresaw the problems of water running into the Fens from the high country via the rivers Nene, the Great Ouse and the Welland. He advocated the use of washes, the embankment of flood areas alongside the rivers, which would hold excess water when the rivers overflowed until such time as they receded, when the waters would be released and discharged into the sea. Westerdyke, another Dutchman and a great rival of Vermuyden, advocated banking the rivers up to hold excess flood water rather than washes. Would they have stood the test of time? We will never know, but one thing we can be certain of is that the washes have worked and proved their worth to fen drainage for nearly 400 years.

Vermuyden's idea of flood washes was not popular, and yet they would become the last bastions of fen life. Here a few of the remaining Fen Tigers (see pages 126–34) could carry on their way of life for the next 300 years unhindered; and the washes would also become a wildfowler's paradise, an ice skater's dream and a grazier's utopia.

The fenland landscape and especially the flood washes were littered with crack willow (*Salix fragilis*) and when pollarded made ideal material for eel hives, baskets, skeps, sheep hurdles and other vessels. It thrives in moist conditions along

A group of young local people in 1930s attire enjoying some social skating on Cowbit Wash.

Top left: Cowbit Wash, 1930s. Two people preparing to skate to music from a portable wind-up gramophone.

Above: Pairs skating on Cowbit Wash, 1930s.

Left: British Professional Champion James Smart skating against 'Young Gutty', at Wisbech on the River Nene in January 1891. (LRC)

watercourses where it also binds the soil and prevents riverbanks slipping or eroding, making it a valuable asset to the fenland management. Cowbit Wash up to the 1960s had a field near the Brother House Bar that was entirely crack willow and every year basket-makers from Spalding, Peterborough and surrounding villages would come and cut the willow for basket-making.

Up to the 1960s potatoes were still picked by hand on the fen farms, an activity requiring many thousands of baskets. In ancient times the roots of crack willow were boiled to produce a purple dye used at Easter to decorate hens' eggs. Osier (*Salix viminalis*) was also common in the flood washes and when coppiced provided withies, an excellent material for baskets, fish traps and furniture. When the flooded washes froze in the winter months the fenman could demonstrate his prowess at speed skating, taking on all comers from outside the area. The seventeenth and eighteenth centuries would see skating matches on a parochial scale but with the advent of the train in the nineteenth century thousands of people from all parts of the country would come to the washes and the remaining meres to skate, some for pleasure, others to compete in the many races held here. The *Cambridge Chronicle* of 2 January 1841 reports more than 6,000 people gathered at Whittlesey Mere to watch a skating match for £10 prize money.

In the minute book of 1728 at the Spalding Gentlemen's Society it is recorded that 'Mr Harrison Baker of the town goes on ice pattens or skates with a velocity and grace equal to a Dutch Hollander, a mile in 3 mins'. Fen people refer to skates as pattens. Skates comes from the Dutch word *schaats*, a word which may have been used by the many Dutch religious refugees who settled in the Fens. The origin of the word 'pattens' for a skate is not certain, but Fen people say it is of French origin from either Norman or Huguenot influence in this area.

Paul and Sally Gotobed repairing fyke nets for catching eels, 1870. (CC)

Below: Making baskets from willows in 1895. (CC)

Possibly another member of the Gotobed family making eel hives from willow. (CC)

Women harvesting osier in the late nineteenth century. (CC)

Stripping willows at a willow yard. (CC)

Harvesting osier in the late nineteenth century. (CC)

William Den, custodian of Rosewell Pits, collecting reeds in a punt for thatching in the late 1880s. (CC)

But for Vermuyden's vision we may have been witnessing the same fate as many of the flooded areas in the country during the past few years. The works carried out between 1600 and 1660 were daunting, even on today's scale, and it has to be remembered that it was all performed with hand labour. Some authors writing on fen drainage, however, have said this period in fen history was not the age of visionaries: I cannot agree. There were many, as we have seen, men such as Sir Cornelius Vermuyden, Sir Philibert Vernatti, Justice Popham, the Russells, Colonel Dodson and two of our kings, James I and Charles I. It was the lack of adequate legislative powers, engendered by the conflict between king and parliament, that hindered the advancement of draining in this country compared to some of the Low Countries in Europe. It was not therefore until the General Drainage Act of 1861, when Drainage Boards of elected members were created, nearly 300 years after the General Sewers Act, that more coordination was brought to fen drainage. The rivers also were under fragmented management until 1930 when River Catchment Boards were formed, and even these did not come under the control of one body until 1990, with the birth of the National Rivers Authority. The seventeenth and eighteenth centuries were fertile years, but they furnished engineers whose schemes were either too ambitious, too controversial or too costly to carry out at the time but which would be revived years later when conditions demanded. Almost all the main drains we have today were invented at this time; and the challenge for mankind to drain the Fens brought together foreigners, religious refugees, the English aristocracy and prisoners of war.

A Poet's Vision of Drained Fens and Marshes

I sing Floods muzled and oceans tam'
Luxurious rivers govern'd and Reclaimed,
Water with Banks confin'd as in a Gaol
Till kinder Sluces let them go to Bail.
Streams curb'd with Dams like Bridles, taught t'obey
And run as strait, as if they saw their way.

There shall a change of Men and Manners be;
Hearts, thick and tough as Hydes, shall feel Remorse,
And souls of Sedge shall understand Discourse,
New hands shall learn to Work, forget to Steal,
New legs shall go to church, new knees shall kneel.
*(popularly attributed to Samuel Fortrey, Director of
Bedford Land Corporation, mid-seventeenth century)*

A New Breed of Fenmen

The drainage schemes of the seventeenth century brought, directly and indirectly, a new breed of fenmen. The work itself had partly been accomplished with the help of Protestant refugees from France and Belgium, skilled people who were mainly of middle-class origin, and Dutch engineers brought over by the first Stuart kings. But in addition to the huge labour force involved the scale of the operations in draining

The eighteenth-century gravestone of a Huguenot man who lived in Thorney. A member of this family married into the Sly family.

the Fens needed professional men to administer and supervise the works, and to farm the large areas of fertile land made available by the new schemes. The adventurers who now owned large areas of the Fen were eager for a return on their investments, and as the large estates did not farm themselves tenants were required. As well as tenants there were opportunities for blacksmiths, weavers, millers, butchers and traders, and people to deal with accounts, legal matters, book keeping and insurance to service this industry. Social and medical needs had to be catered for, too, calling in the need for surgeons, veterinary surgeons, physicians, teachers, preachers and shopkeepers. Many other professions and trades were also required. There were many breweries in the Fens before the drainage schemes got under way – Elgoods of Wisbech, for example – but more were established as a result. Bankers arrived to cash in on the boom that had been created. One such person was Jonathan Peckover, a Quaker from the higher ground in Norfolk, who came to Wisbech and built Peckover House.

Trade in and out of the Fens by ship had been carried on since the Romans were here and since then had slowly increased. King's Lynn, Boston, Wisbech and Spalding were the major ports during this period, and all except Spalding are still in

Sailing ships moored in Wisbech Port in the late nineteenth century. (LRC)

Ships moored in Wisbech Port in the twentieth century. (LRC)

use today. Before the expansion of the British Empire in the eighteenth century and the sudden growth of western ports such as Liverpool, the east coast ports were vital to Britain's trade. In the thirteenth century the port of Boston was second only to London and boasted no less than sixteen guilds.

Education also prospered as an indirect result of the drainage schemes. From the thirteenth to the eighteenth century Fen towns and ports grew not only into thriving places for trade and business but as social centres and meeting places for the intelligentsia. In the medieval period the abbeys had been centres of education and religious teaching, taking in sons of noble families in particular, and as there were no other teaching establishments schools grew up around the Fens. The city of Ely, founded when the first abbey was built in 673, can boast one of the oldest teaching establishments in the country. The *Liber Eliensis* states that people of the highest rank brought their children to be educated there. From early times the school had close links with St John's College, Peterhouse and Jesus College, Cambridge, all founded by former bishops of Ely. Henry VIII refounded the school as King's School to teach young men grammar as well as scripture in 1541, and so today it is known as King's Ely. The school finances were somewhat depleted in 1636 when monies bequeathed by Dean Caesar to the school were lent by Archbishop Laud to Charles I to be repaid with interest: these were never recovered. The small town of Wainfleet in the northern part of the Fens also has a bond with Magdalen College, Oxford, owing its foundation in 1484 to William Patten, alias William of Waynflete. Waynflete became bishop of Winchester and Lord Chancellor of England as well as founding Winchester College and helping in the foundation of Eton College. He was without doubt one of the country's greatest educationalists and patrons of learning of late medieval England. The grammar school in Wainfleet was founded by him in 1460 and endowed with a house for the master to live in, together with an income from Magdalen College revenues. The

The porters' lodge at King's Ely, one of the oldest schools in the kingdom. (RS)

Wainfleet Grammar School, founded in 1484 by William of Wainfleet and now a museum and library. (RS)

Boston Grammar School was built in 1567 and is still used as the school library. (RS)

school remained a grammar school until it was transferred to nearby Skegness in 1933. Wainfleet played an active role in the administration and running of Tattershall College, north of Boston, between 1450 and 1480. Fountains Abbey, in North Yorkshire, like several other religious houses, owned property in Wormgate Street in Boston and had established a school there before 1325.

Although throughout the country many people in search of work had moved into the growing industrial cities, there still remained many impoverished people in and around the Fens in the late seventeenth and eighteenth centuries. In 1677 an order proclaimed that if anyone brought people to live and work in the Fen, and those people became poor and unable to maintain themselves, then they should be the responsibility of the employer who brought them in and not of the undertakers as a whole. Undertakers were occasionally reminded of this. In 1744 the adventurers considered it necessary to instruct Grundy to do away with all vagrants coming into the Fens chargeable to themselves. In 1759 the adventurers paid £119 towards keeping paupers.

Vast numbers of prisoners had been brought into the Fens for manual work during the seventeenth century, but as soon as the work ran out their presence engendered poverty and hardship. Place names sometimes reflect this: in 1832 improvised labour was employed when a drain was cut to straighten a detour below Kindersley's Cut on the Nene; the area was named Paupers Cut. More evidence of the use of prisoners can be found at Norman's Cross near Peterborough, which was a French prisoner of war camp between 1793 and 1815, housing 6,272 prisoners – by way of comparison, the population of Peterborough at that time was 4,075. The buildings of the camp alone covered 22 acres, and the whole site 42 acres. Typhoid was rampant here and the nearby cemetery has 1,770 graves, 1,020 of which were for prisoners who had died of this disease between 1800 and 1801. It is more than likely that these men had been brought in to dig the drains that were being cut across the Fens, especially in the Thorney area, at this time.

THE SPALDING GENTLEMEN'S SOCIETY

During the seventeenth and eighteenth centuries a great many aristocratic families owned land in the Fens, including the Dukes of Buccleuch, Bedford and Lancaster, the Marquis of Exeter, the Lords Carrington, Kesteven and Normanton, the Earls of Lindsey, Lincoln, Fitzwilliam and many more. Two of the estates of Gideon Sampson (1699–1762), a capitalist and financier of Portuguese Jewish origin who accumulated a large fortune and invested heavily in land, were in the Fens, near Spalding and Peterborough. In 1745 he freely lent his property and his credit to the government, and raised a loan of £1,700,000 when the French fleet held the Channel and the government's funds were falling.

Sampson was one of the early members of the Spalding Gentlemen's Society, one of the oldest learned societies in the land, founded in 1710 by Maurice Johnson, the antiquary of Ayscoughfee Hall, Spalding. It began with a series of informal meetings of a few local gentlemen at a coffee house in Abbey Yard to discuss local antiquities and to read the *Tatler*, the newly established London periodical. As the meetings progressed it was decided to establish a society on a more formal basis and to broaden its intellectual interests for discussions, at the same time appointing officers to take minutes. Francis, Duke of Buccleuch, Lord of the Manor of

Spalding, became a Patron of the Society in 1732 and the present Duke of Buccleuch and Queensbury is Patron of the Society today. Maurice Johnson was a member of the Royal Society in London (founded in 1663) and with the help of William Stukeley wished to emulate such a society in Spalding. The formation of the society illustrates the type of people active in the Fens at this time. Early members included Sir Isaac Newton, Sir Hans Sloane, President of the Royal Society, Alexander Pope, George Vertue, Dr William Stukeley, John Anstis, John Gray, John Perry, Samuel Wesley, Sir Edward Bellamy and Lord Coleraine. Other distinguished members after the founder's death were Sir Joseph Banks, Sir George Gilbert Scott, Alfred Lord Tennyson, Pishey Thompson, Lord Curzon of Kedleston, who restored Tattershall Castle and bequeathed it to the National Trust, and Lord Peckover, to name but a few. The Society has its own museum, housing a wealth of antiquities amassed over a period of 300 years by gifts, bequests and purchases, and a library with a fine collection of interesting and rare books. Today the Society is still flourishing, with over 300 members who meet to discuss local antiquities and other matters of interest and listen to lectures once a fortnight during the winter months. People of standing and learning have thus come to Spalding to the Society for over 300 years, to attend or give lectures or to use the Society's archives for research. The Society is one of the most treasured legacies of the Fenland's past.

EARLY PIONEERS

One man we have to thank for much valuable information on the Fens and its drainage of this period is Sir William Dugdale, who wrote the *History of Imbanking*

Sir William Dugdale, whose valuable history of Fen drainage in the sixteenth and seventeenth centuries is treasured by modern historians.

and Draining of the divers Fens and Marshes both in Foreign Parts and this Kingdom. It is a most valuable chronicle of this era and to many fen people it is their Bible, precious copies handed down through the family to be enjoyed by successive generations, never to be sold. Dugdale was employed by the Honourable Corporation of Bedford Level as a clerk from as early as 1643 and published his book some nine years later, in 1651. Edward, Lord Gorges, adventurer, Director of Works and later Surveyor General for the Corporation, had requested Dugdale to document work done by the Corporation and others to further the cause for future drainage. The book not only covers fen and marsh drained in this area but also similar low-lying areas of Kent, Somerset and the isle of Axholme in north Lincolnshire.

During the eighteenth century little advancement was made in fen drainage and flood defence, with few major schemes introduced compared to the mammoth ones undertaken by the adventurers in the previous century. Small improvements were carried out, but the problem of low-lying land, much of it shrinking, at great distances away from the outfalls still remained a problem. The artificial movement of water relied on wind power to drive scoopwheels – a somewhat precarious method of propulsion – and so until larger and more efficient pumping systems were invented to lift water into the drains, flooding would recur. Even more critical to the whole concept of draining the Fens were the river outfalls.

While neither of these problems were unknown the latter had not been considered in depth. The main rivers discharging into the Wash, the Witham, the Welland, the Nene, the Great Ouse and the Glen (which ran into the Welland), would have to be dealt with. What had made the problem worse was the enclosing of large areas of marsh in the seventeenth century, when the old tidal rivers such as the Whaplode, Moulton, Holbeach and Fleet as well as Gosberton and Bicker Haven had become less important as drainage channels, which meant that the main rivers had to cope with more water, with poor maintenance and still no unified body to supervise management, a problem that would take another hundred years to achieve.

John Grundy (1719–83) was influential during this period in the draining of Deeping Fen and the Witham Improvement, while his son, also John, carried on in his father's footsteps. In the early eighteenth century it had proved impossible to prevent flooding in Deeping Fen, despite the efforts of Thomas Lovell in 1603 and Captain John Perry in 1734. Perry bought a large part of Deeping Fen from a group of adventurers who had not been receiving rent, owing to the poor condition of the farms there, and in return could not pay their taxes to parliament. He was unsuccessful in curing the outfall problem of the Venatt's Drain and the Welland through and below Spalding. John Grundy Senior did much work on both watercourses but the problem would not be completely solved until after the major floods of 1947, some 200 years later. John Grundy Junior carried on his father's work in Deeping Fen.

In the year 1751 Nathaniel Kinderley brought forward a scheme for the improvement of the Great Fen rivers discharging into the estuary, joining them all up as one, which turned out to be only a dream. His son Charles Kinderley continued this work, suggesting the straightening of many fen rivers, especially the Great Ouse at King's Lynn and the Nene from Wisbech to the outfall. Improvements were carried out on the Nene between Crab's Holt and the South Holland sluice (known as Kinderley's Cut), and finally completed between 1773 and 1795, only solving a small part of the problem on this river. Breaches of the north bank of the Nene in 1763, 1764, 1767 and 1770 had strengthened the hand of those who wished the outfall improved and in 1773 the Tydd and Newton Drainage Bill was presented to parliament. On 3 May Wisbech Corporation accepted the Bill and asked John Grundy to give his opinion on the scheme and draw up such clauses as he thought necessary for the security of their trade and navigation.

An extract from *The Life of John Grundy Engineer* highlights the problems that beset drainage schemes: 'For fifty years since 1720 there has been litigation and argument between Wisbech Corporation and those interested in the drainage of the North Level of the Fens concerning the outfall of the river Nene.' Legal disputes, the lack of coordinated organisation and adequate governmental legislation were, without doubt, the main stumbling blocks in improving the drainage progress in Britain during this period, and later. Much of the work in drainage and flood defences involved lawyers acting for various owners from all parts of England and Scotland. Discussions, debates and legal wrangling between rival interests often took longer and proved more costly at times than the works themselves. The securing of the necessary Acts of Parliament also hindered works, although this was lucrative for the legal profession. It would be an interesting exercise to compare expenditure on legal fees and administration between 1600 and 1900 with expenditure involved in the drainage work itself!

A great engineer and surveyor of national standing was John Smeaton, who in 1767 made a report on Denver Sluice. The original sluice built by Vermuyden in the 1640s had blown up in 1713 when high spring tides met high country floodwater coming down the Old Bedford River. This sluice had caused much controversy from the time it was built, not only from the landowners upstream of it but also from the owners of boats transporting cargo along the river. A new sluice was built, however, between 1748 and 1750, under the supervision of an eminent Swiss engineer, Charles Labelye, that would last until 1821. Denver was not the only sluice to cause controversy: the Grand Sluice at Boston did likewise, and in fact many other sluices across the Fens proved constant sources of conflict. The problem lay partly in the materials used – they were built of wood – and partly in the conflicting interests between the people who wanted to drain the Fens and the lightermen whose living depended on the waterways operating their lighters on the river to convey freight. This difficulty would remain until stone, brick and steel were used in their construction, but more importantly the river outfalls would have to be improved, requiring major schemes to be undertaken.

The Grand Sluice of 1765 at Boston controlled the waters of the Black Sluice, an area still prone to flooding, and was replaced by the new one in 1846, the basis of which remains today. This enabled large improvements to be made to low-lying land in this area, and yet it would take another hundred years for it to be declared drained.

In the early nineteenth century wind pumps were superseded by the beam engine powered by steam, but even this modern invention was not able to cope with increased demand for drainage. By 1820 the first beam engines were used in the Fens to drive scoopwheels. The early ones were small, not more than 20 hp, but by 1830 engines of 80 hp were being used to drive scoopwheels of up to 50 feet in diameter. At the Great Exhibition of 1851 in London the Appold centrifugal pump was on show for the first time, and it was this new invention, together with the steam engine, that was to revolutionise fen drainage. Wheeler mentions a

One of the last remaining wind pumps at Turf Fen, 1910. (CC)

A 40-paddle scoopwheel over 20 feet in diameter under construction. It would have been driven by a steam-powered beam engine. (CC)

Stretham Pump House, which houses a working steam beam engine and scoopwheel. (RS)

An old pumphouse converted for use as a private dwelling. RS)

A pumphouse on Bevill's Leam. It would have housed a steam-driven beam engine in the nineteenth century. (RS)

pumping station at Lade Bank in East Fen in 1867 with two Appold's centrifugal pumps worked by steam engines, and at Bourne Fen a Butterley condensing steam engine of 30 hp driving an iron scoopwheel 15 feet in diameter and consuming 2½ tons of coal a day. A map of the Black Sluice area dated 1856 shows nine steam and eight wind-drainage machines, draining an area of approximately 18,000 acres.

There are two excellent examples of these pumping stations at Pinchbeck near Spalding and Stretham near Ely, both cared for by devoted enthusiasts.

THE GOLDEN ERA OF FEN DRAINAGE

In the period following the Industrial Revolution, the landed gentry keen to acquire more land and businessmen still known as adventurers invested fortunes to fund massive drainage works in the Fens. Engineers now had at their disposal the power of steam, modern engineering techniques and lessons learnt from the industrial age. With new pumps, imaginative ideas and new materials they were ready to do battle with the elements. There was renewed interest in drainage in this period, brought about largely by the developments of the Industrial Revolution, and many of the great engineers of this era were keen to take on the challenge of draining the Fens in one part or another. Innovative engineers such as Grundy, William Lewin, Stevenson, Sir William Cubitt, Thomas Telford, Smeaton, Mylne, Labelye, Brunel, Robert Hawkesleya, William Henry Wheeler and Coode all had involvement in draining the Fens.

Perhaps one of the greatest engineers of this era was Sir John Rennie, who designed and advised on drainage schemes through the whole of the Fens. He, like Vermuyden 200 years before him, could see that the major obstacle in draining the Fens was the river outfalls into the Wash. Unless the Witham, the Nene, the Great Ouse and the Welland outfalls were improved by major works, the use of modern pumps would be wasted. Colonel Dodson, an adventurer in the early days of draining the Fens, commented on Vermuyden's first scheme that 'in all draining we have respect for our Out-fall, and if we cannot be master there, all other endeavours signify nothing.' All these rivers had over the past century been gradually silting up, making the discharge of high country and fen water difficult, while at the same time hindering the movement of water traffic.

In 1839 Sir John Rennie suggested a scheme for draining by fascine* the rivers Ouse, Nene, Welland and Witham into one common outfall at the centre of the Wash, enclosing 150,000 acres of land. The scheme was found to be impracticable and the powers obtained were allowed to lapse; however the Lincolnshire Estuary Company was formed and the Welland and Witham were improved to discharge into Boston Deeps. Rennie also advised on the improvements to the Nene and the Eau Brink outfall of the River Ouse, both these works being carried out successfully by Joliffe and Banks in the 1830s. In 1830 Messrs Rennie and Telford devised a scheme for straightening the River Nene from Kinderley's Cut to Crab Holt, at a cost of £200,716, carried out by Joliffe and Banks and called Nene Outfall Cut. Tyco Wing (the Duke of Bedford's agent), son of John Wing, was also influential in this scheme which would have great benefits to their Thorney estate.

Railways came into the Fens in the mid-nineteenth century, criss-crossing the drains and rivers over bridges of steel and brick. Road bridges were also built of cast iron, stone, brick and wood, many of which remain today in excellent condition. The increase in traffic brought about by the turnpikes encouraged major bridge-building throughout the country during the late eighteenth century and into the nineteenth. The General Highways Acts allowed magistrates to make indictments in respect of bridges, thus rendering the counties more responsible for their condition.

There are many relics of this golden era across the Fens, for it was a revolutionary period in fenland history. Tyco Wing left his mark with a three-arch bridge and

---

* A fascine was a long faggot, usually of hawthorn or willow, bundled together with string or willow to form a mattress for bank and bed protection, or creating a bed for a drain or river. It often rested on a stone base.

Cow Bridge footbridge over the Maud Foster Drain, Boston, built by Sir John Rennie in 1811. Grade II listed, it is made of cast-iron with a single-span arch of open-framed voussoirs cast at Butterley. (RS)

Two-Plank Bridge over Vernatti's drain. (RS)

Frieston Bridge near Boston. A three-arch bridge of brick construction with stone copings on the abutments and parapets. It was built by Sir John Rennie, as were many others that remain in this area. (RS)

sluice at Clough Cross as well as several single-arch brick bridges with round pillars over each abutment. A three-arch cast-iron bridge stands in front of the sluice at the outfall of the North Level Drain near Tydd. This was cast and erected by Grissell and Co. of London in 1866 and has stood against two tides a day for nearly 130 years. Nearby at Sutton Bridge the 850-ton swing bridge made by Armstrong Whitworth and Co. can still be seen, originally powered by water from a nearby accumulator now converted to hydraulics.

Bluegowt Outfall. A brick-built bridge with flap doors that allow water to flow one way only. This eighteenth-century bridge is on the River Glen near Surfleet Seas End. Gowt and gote are Saxon words for sluice. (RS)

Hopkins First World War portable bridge erected by the Middle Level Commissioners in 1920, spanning a fen drain. The bridge has a span of 120 feet and is capable of carrying First World War tanks. (RS)

Trinity Bridge, Crowland, built between 1360 and 1390. This bridge stands in the centre of the village and would have been used by pack horses and pedestrians. The River Welland flowed under it some 350 years ago, from where it was diverted to the abbey and the Nene. For centuries it has been a meeting place for the elders of Crowland. Today it is classed as an Ancient Monument. (RS)

As well as bridges there are many magnificent sluices built during the period that also serve as bridges, all part of the fenland scene. Many old and new pumping stations exist as well. The town of Boston and the Witham Fourth Internal Drainage Boards have fine examples of Rennie's bridges in brick and iron. The first bridge that he built in England was at Boston Bargate in 1803, while two of his elegant footbridges span the Maud Foster drain today. There are also many of his brick bridges, single- and double-arch, not forgetting the three-arched bridge at Freiston. Spalding and Market

Deeping both boast fine stone bridges from this period and there are the three stone bridges along the Roman Cardyke between Bourne and Peterborough.

Even with man's modern inventions and technology it would again be legislation and political wrangling that would stem the tide of progress. The Bedford Level Corporation formed in 1663 was losing its control and influence throughout the Bedford Level. The North Level had been partially removed from its control in 1753 but it would take a hundred years before the Middle and South Level Commissions would be fully incorporated as separate bodies (accomplished in 1861). As late as 1868 W.H. Wheeler thought the number of private acts of parliament in force in relation to the Witham, Welland, Nene, and Great Ouse 'extraordinary'. He deplored a situation where the 'number of jurisdictions which have control over the river or the banks has accumulated till at times it is almost impossible to define their powers and rights'.

Above: Wiggenhall St Germans sluice was built in 1844 and blown up in 1862.

Right: Wiggenhall St Germans dam being constructed after the old sluice was blown out by water pressure in 1862.

Men cleansing the South Forty Foot Drain in 1910.

A gang of drainers pose for a photograph after cutting a new drain in the late nineteenth or early twentieth century.

A gang using shovels and clay barrows, which were wheeled on barrow roads. The filled barrows were wheeled to a crossing point where another man would wheel it to the next.

The eighteenth and nineteenth centuries brought hundreds of Acts of Parliament granting permission to improve the rivers and their outfalls, cut new drains and enclose common land in the Fens and the out marshes, which would shape the future of fen drainage. The Land Drainage Act of 1847, reverting to the old practice regarding the early statutory sewers, enabled the king to grant, on the recommendation of the Enclosure Commissioners, commissions of sewers to different parts of the country. Such commissions were appointed and were entitled to exercise certain powers of cleaning and repairing or deepening and improving drains, and also to carry out the construction of new ones, or, when any district preferred to run the business independently, on the basis of an elective body, the Act provided for the constitution of Elective Drainage Boards.

This led to the General Drainage Act of 1861, a milestone in drainage legislation, creating drainage boards of elected members, and hundreds of large and small drainage boards, many of which remain today. These had the powers to borrow money for drainage in their area and levy rates subject to valuation, which is still the basis of today's system. Wheeler states that

> Under this drainage act, Commissions of Sewers may, with the approval of the Enclosure Commissioners, be issued for districts where they have not formerly existed, if it can be shown that the state of the drainage district is such as to require some controlling body to superintend the outfalls. However, as this Act gives the option between a Commission or an Elected Drainage District it is the latter that carries out this duty now.

The court of sewers is not only an ancient but very important body of commissioners, with responsibilities and extensive powers. They can summon juries, administer oaths, set rates, levy fines and issue distresses. Many of their Acts are judicial, and can only be set aside by appeals to the high courts. Much of the drainage work was now carried out by the Internal Drainage Boards. But there are still a few parishes that do not rely on sewers*, gotes** and sluices of the Court of Sewers for their drainage.

* Ancient word for small river or drain carrying water to the sea.
** Saxon term, later gowt, for a sluice that allows fresh water to exit a sluice but keeps out sea water.

In 1877 a select committee of the House of Lords was set up to enquire into the formation of drainage authorities. It advocated that each catchment area be placed under a single body of conservators, to be responsible for maintaining the rivers from source to outfall. This would have been a major advance at a time when the river outfalls still jeopardised the whole of the fen drainage systems, but it was not to be.

It would not be long however – some twenty years after the Corn Laws had been repealed in1846 – that farming, and therefore life in the Fens, would descend into the longest depression in its history, lasting until the First World War. The Corn Laws were repealed owing to pressure from industrialists and workers for cheaper food from abroad, and to this extent the measure was a success – grain and meat flooded in from North and South America, Argentina, Australia and New Zealand. But these imports undercut the British farmer. The period that followed, known as the great depression, is still remembered in the Fens, where there was no other way of making a living other than farming; and yet the time would come when farmers were needed again to feed the nation during the two world wars.

Fenland farms were small, usually owned by large estates but farmed by tenants, unlike many of the large estates outside the Fens, which were farmed by the owners themselves. In 1851, 7,000 people owned 80 per cent of the land in Britain, and status was still assessed in acres: if you owned between 100 and 1,000 acres you were considered a yeoman; to own between 1,000 and 10,000 acres qualified you as a member of the gentry and if you owned over 10,000 acres you were deemed an aristocrat. There might have been the odd yeoman in the Fens, but most of the land was owned by the gentry and the aristocracy.

A contemporary source commented:

> During the great agricultural depression village life has changed, abandoned cottages, derelict windmills were to be seen, wheel-wrights, blacksmiths, carpenters, masons, coach-makers, have all declined, the symbol of a declining rural industry. Local habits and amusements disappear together with local dishes, dialects, feasts, fairs, wakes and longstanding customs . . . village life will never be the be the same again.

Ironically, these words are being uttered again today across the whole of the United Kingdom. Although a kind of village life did survive this first depression, I believe those words will come to fruition in the next half-century.

THE BEDFORDS

The 6th Duke of Bedford (1769–1839) was the first governor of the Agricultural Society in 1838, and developed the land around the village of Thorney into a model agricultural estate second to none in the land. During this period huge schemes were carried out, modern beam engines driven by steam, driving firstly, scoopwheels then centrifugal pumps. New sluices were erected and many drains cut employing the finest engineers such as Telford and Rennie. The Duke's agent Tyco Wing, who

Portsand Bridge, French Drove, Thorney. This bridge and many like it in the Thorney area were built in 1833 when the Duke of Bedford carried out extensive drainage works on his estate. Grade II listed, it is brick-built with round abutments with coping stones and iron parapets. (RS)

was influential in the Nene outfall of 1830, stated in evidence before a committee of the House of Lords in 1848 that 'the value of land in some parts of the North Level had increased 100%, and in some cases more, and it is well known that land that might have been bought twenty years ago for £5 per acre, would now bring from £60 to £70'. The tenants on the estate had experienced a reasonably stable income, which encouraged the Bedford family to invest in the estate. The repeal of the Corn Laws in 1846 allowing free access to agricultural goods from around the world to feed the growing industrial population would put paid to that. Farming, however, did not suffer the recession until about twenty years after that event.

With the repeal of the Corn Laws and the subsequent farming depression, the demise of the Bedford Thorney estate began. It was the 11th Duke (1858–1940), after the family fortunes had been somewhat depleted, who sold off the last acres of the Thorney estate in 1930, ending 400 hundred years of the Russell family's involvement in the Fens. The irony of this precious legacy to the fen dweller is that the Bedford family probably lost more money creating this estate than they ever made out of it. When their vision for draining the Fens had finally been achieved they were forced to sell those precious acres at a time when land values were at their lowest for decades and tenants struggling for their very existence. It was a sad end to a family whose earls and dukes for 400 years had been so devoted to the drainage of the Fens, the welfare of its people and the quality of its farms.

The Bedfords have left their mark in the Great Level of the Fens in perpetuity, farms, houses, drains, bridges, sluices as well as Bedford Hall and Thorney village, all created in the seventeenth to nineteenth centuries by these visionaries of the

Bedford Hall, Thorney. Originally the water works for the village and estate offices built in the mid-nineteenth century, it is now used as a Heritage Centre and Village Hall. (RS)

Above: Nineteenth-century houses in Thorney village. The estate as we know it today was developed while Francis, 7th Duke of Bedford, held the title (1839–61). (RS)

Herbrand, 11th Duke of Bedford. He sold the Thorney estate in the early twentieth century. (By kind permission of the Marquess of Tavistock and the Trustees of the Bedford Estate)

past. Thorney was in many respects a model village and is described in detail in Miller and *Fenland Past and Present*:

> Everything about it seems under careful supervision. There are good elementary schools; no children are seen loitering on the road during school hours, and those in the school look well-clad, cheerful and healthy . . . as there is provision for rational amusement and mental culture – and how can a community develop in real manhood when these are entirely wanting? There are reading rooms supplied with daily papers, periodicals, and books; a lecture room comfortably fitted and ventilated, and a working men's club in the course of formation, all carried on with due regard to the principles of local self government; while the temptation to drinking habits is reduced to a minimum. Here we found waterworks, sewage works, and gas works. All cottages are lighted with gas, have water taps, a good arrangement for carrying off wastewater, and in about two thirds of them the earth closet is employed.
>
> Every cottage has a good garden and may have a plot of ground of half an acre at a small rental, the death rate is 16 per 1,000. Travellers going on the Midland Railway from Peterborough to Wisbech may see a large building, with a tower, standing between the railway and Thorney Abbey. In the tower is a reservoir to hold 10,000 gallons of water, and from this the village is supplied. The water comes into the estate from the Nene and runs up the 'Thorney river' to be purified by filtration where it is pumped into the reservoir. In the building referred to there are two fine engines each of 25 hp, they are employed for pumping the water, and also the sewage which is used for irrigation. In the same building are spacious workshops and storerooms containing the necessary appliances for keeping things in order. We have no analysis of the water, and we are satisfied that it is well filtered and that the filter beds are periodically cleaned, yet we know that it is river water; however we observed a liberal supply of tanks placed above the ground for catching rain water.

This brief note on Thorney may not convey to the reader an adequate idea of what the village is really like: to any who wish to know more there is only one solution – to make a visit themselves. The above account was written when clean water was difficult to obtain in the Fens. Miller and Skertchly also commented on towns such as March, Whittlesey and Peterborough, which had inferior water quality. That at King's Lynn was variable while Boston and Spalding were supplied with good water from the high country. Towns and villages farthest away from the high country where springs or artesian wells were not found were the worst off.

WHITTLESEY MERE

Until the end of the eighteenth century there were still many meres in the Fens, the main ones being Whittlesey, Ugg, Soham, Stretham and Ramsey, all in the south. In the northern section there were many small meres grouped together called 'the

Deeps', lying in West Fen, north of Boston. All had been drained by the beginning of the nineteenth century or had dried up on account of the drainage carried out around them. Whittlesey Mere, an area of between 1,000 and 2,000 acres, had been shrinking and drying up since land had been drained in the surrounding fens and moors. Its life would come to an end in 1851 when it was finally drained, and man had achieved his goal – or so he thought! The area flooded the next year but with the new tools of the industrial age, steam and steel, fenmen finally triumphed and tamed the last fen monster. This was less than one hundred years after Sir Charles Ordford had made his epic journey across the Fens with a flotilla of six boats, much of his time having been spent on Whittlesey Mere. He recorded his journey and travels in *Lord Orford's Voyage round the Fens in 1774*, describing the land, the mere and the people living there, which gives an excellent insight into life at that time. King Canute had sailed here, regattas and skating matches had been held, and fish was caught in abundance. But all this was to end because of man's ambition to drain every inch of this ancient part of the Fens with his new inventions. The draining of Whittlesey and nearby Ugg Mere as well as many other smaller meres – mainly through drains such as Bevill's Leam, which ran into the Nene at Rings End, and Vermuyden's drain running to the Great Ouse – would bring large areas of moor into cultivation at the same time. The moorlands* of the southern Fens, of White Moor, Glass Moor, West Moor, Binnimoor, How Moor, Dyke Moor, Horse Moor, Ranson Moor and many others formed vast areas of black peat between Whittlesey, Rings End and Chatteris, accumulated over thousands of years.

Much has been made of the draining of the meres and their loss to the fenland ecosystem, but the loss of the moors with its islands and small lakes was far greater. The names are still to be seen on Ordnance Survey maps to remind us of what was here before we changed the fen moorlands. It is fascinating to study a map of this area of the Fens: every drain, moor, mere and fen is documented by a name, every farm a record of history. This area was dotted with hills, maybe only a few feet above the floodline but nevertheless a safe haven for men, livestock, fauna and flora, and each telling its own tale. Horsey Hill, Honey Hill, Brown's Hill, Amber Hill and Suet Hills and even more aloof Ramsey Heights. There are some areas that are not fens or meres, such as the Turves, King's Delph (after King John), Copalder, Bodsey, Puddock (a Scottish toad), Eldernell, Wype Doles, Bishops' Lands and Adventurers' Lands, Botany Bay, and the Rakes. One could study, analyse and document every part of the Fens yet still leave many questions unanswered.

Man (my ancestors included) has won from nature every part of this land at some time in the past for his own ends. Even during the late nineteenth-century depression the urge to drain land for agricultural use was still dominant. In 1878 Samuel Miller and Sydney Skertchley stated in *The Fenland Past and Present* that 'Newly re-claimed peat-land is of comparatively little value' owing to its large

---

* Old English *mor* is cognate with Saxon *moer*, meaning swamp, while Indo-European *moro*, or standing water, is also related to mere.

quantity of acid. Was there a moral reason to drain the last great fen mere for crops with so much cheap food available? The economic reasons were even less sustainable with the British Empire at its zenith and cheap food available from all corners of the world. If this were to happen today there would be a worldwide outcry. The conservation groups, the media and any other preservation lobby groups would jump on the bandwagon. Politicians and pop stars would thrive on it for publicity and moral issues and yet there are probably more humans on the breadline now than there were in the middle of the eighteenth century. If morals are so important in the annals of our conscience it could be said that the Wash should be drained and farmed to feed the starving peoples of the third world.

> These Fens have often times by water drown'd,
> Science in remedy in water found,
> The power of steam she said shall be employed,
> And the destroyer by itself destroyed.
> *(Inscription on the Hundred drain pumping station near Pry Moor, 1830)*

UGG MILL

The mill is situated aproximately three-quarters of a mile west of Ramsey St Mary on the south side of the old River Nene. During its working life it was owned by the Middle Level Commissioners, but it is now privately owned. The size of the mill suggests it would have driven a very large scoopwheel. At the north side are the foundations of what was a steam-powered beam engine that was used after the mill became redundant, probably when Ugg Mere was drained in 1850–60. The beam engine was still in operation up to 1930, pumping water from Ugg Mere and Lotting Fen into the old Nene. Because of the shrinkage of the peat the land continuously sank and the pump was not able to work efficiently and so was made redundant. Ugg Mill is probably the last remaining relic to remind us of that turning-point in fen drainage history when steam superseded wind power.

Ugg Mill which pumped water from Ugg Mere into the Old Nene up to 1852. It originally housed a scoopwheel driven by a wind engine, then a steam engine. (RS)

CHAPTER THREE

The Wash:
The Fenman's Last Challenge

Fenmen and drainage engineers have for generations gazed at the Wash with possessive eyes, seeing it as their last great challenge to extend their kingdom in the only direction they knew.

One such person was Nathaniel Kinderley, whose son Charles had successfully improved the Nene outfall by cutting Kinderley's Cut.

Of his scheme for the Wash, referring to the fact that the outfall waters of the Nene, the Ouse, the Witham, and the Welland, the four rivers which empty into the estuary, were seriously impeded by the shifting sands which were being continually washed about by the tides, Kinderley says:

> But what do we propose to do with these pernicious sands? Do we think to remove them? No, certainly, that would be quite an impracticable scheme; but though we can't remove them, we may certainly desert them, and if we don't we may be assured that the sea in time will desert us.

He therefore proposed to bring the Nene into the Ouse by a new cut through marshland, and these rivers, when united, were to be carried to the sea under Wooton and Wolverton through the marshes, and to discharge themselves into the deeps by Snettisham. The Welland was to be taken by a new channel inland from about Fossdyke, in the direction of Wyberton, to the Witham, near Skirbeck Quarter, and to continue in a straight course through the country to some convenient place over against Wrangle or Friskney. The result of this he considered would be the entire silting up of the estuary and the gaining of 100,000 acres, the whole of which would become good land in the course of fifty years, 'a new habitable country, 15 miles long and from 8 to 10 in breadth'. Across this new-formed country he proposed that a road should be made, connecting Lynn and Boston. The cost was estimated at £150,000. The waters were thus to be carried in confined channels by the nearest route, direct into deep water. The inadequacy of the estimate for this gigantic scheme will be realised by a reference to the fact that the improvement of the Witham Outfall alone has cost more than this amount.

In the year 1837 a meeting of landowners and others interested in the drainage of lands which had their outfalls into the Wash was held in London, the principal object being the improvement of the River Ouse. As a result of this conference, Sir John Rennie was directed to make a survey and report as to the best means of effecting the improvement. Accordingly, in the following year he began his survey, but it was not completed until the summer of 1839. Rennie suggested that one general scheme for the improvement of the whole of the estuary was far preferable to partial measures; he therefore recommended that the channels of the four rivers should be confined by fascine work, and be led to one common outlet, and that the land should be embanked as it accreted.

Referring to the two rivers which are more particularly dealt with here, he remarked that the Welland and Witham outfalls, particularly the former, were then in a very defective state, and he suggested that they might be improved by either carrying them across the Clays into Clayhole, or by the Maccaroni or South Channel, to join the Nene and Ouse. The advantage of the former plan was that the distance to deep water would be considerably shorter, and in consequence it would be sooner effected; and that custom had hitherto pointed out Boston Deeps as the natural entrance or roadstead both for the Witham and the Welland. On the other hand, looking forward to one general plan and the prospect of maintaining the general outfall open, he thought that there could be little doubt that the greater the body or mass of fresh and tidal water that could be brought into one channel, the greater the certainty of its being able to maintain itself open. In order to effect this enlarged view of the subject, the junctions of the Witham and Welland, Nene and Ouse, into one common outfall, in the centre of the great Wash, appeared the best and most certain plan; and he thought that if the Witham and the Welland were to be carried separately into Clayhole Channel, the Nene into Lynn Well, and the Ouse along the Norfolk shore, there would be a far greater quantity of embankments to make, the channels, by being separate, would not be able to maintain themselves open so well; the land gained would be divided into several separate islands, which would render it more difficult of access, and consequently of less value, while the expense of acquiring it would be greater; and lastly, the boundaries of the counties of Lincoln and Norfolk would be disturbed. The quantity of land that he considered would be gained by the union of four rivers in one common outfall was 150,000 acres. This he estimated as being worth, in a few years, £40 per acre, or a total of £6,000,000, which, after deducting £12 per acre for the expense of obtaining the greater portion, and £15 per acre for that portion lying nearest to the open ocean, together amounting to the sum of £2,000,000, left a clear gain of £4,000,000. This report was presented to a meeting held in London in July 1839, of which Lord George Bentinck was chairman; and it was then resolved, after adopting the report, and expressing the desirability of carrying on the work, 'that the execution of the same must necessarily exceed the means of private individuals, and ought therefore to receive grave consideration and the eventual support of Her Majesty's Government, as a purely national object'. And it was decided further that, although it appeared that great improvements would be made in the various rivers and drainage of land, 'the Promoters of the undertaking do not feel it necessary to call either upon the Land-owners or the parties interested in the navigation for any contribution in the shape of tax or tonnage duty, but will rest satisfied with the reimbursement of their expenses by the acquisition of the

Whittlesey Wash in flood in the late 1990s. This wash has continually flooded since it was constructed by Vermuyden in the seventeenth century, thereby relieving the River Nene of excess flood water. (RS)

land they expect to reclaim from the sea'. But as it proved impossible to raise the funds, no attempt was made to carry out the scheme.

That the Wash is gradually filling up there can be no question, and it is only a matter of time until the bay will be converted into dry land. The bay was once co-extensive with the Fenland itself, and 1,300 square miles have become dry ground within recent geological times – and the process is still going on. Some twenty years ago it was proposed to reclaim most of this wide area, and, as is well known locally, this general scheme fell through owing to local opposition. In the 1960s another project appeared which proposed the Wash Barrage for fresh water storage. With an expanding population and industry spreading into the east and south-east of the country there was an increased demand for water. The scheme was to consider the possibilities of collecting fresh water from the rivers running into the Wash behind a barrage built across the Wash from Fosdyke to King's Lynn. A barrage enclosing the entire Wash was thought beyond the capabilities of existing engineering technology and so four separate reservoirs were proposed instead, covering an area of 25,000 acres, that is, 15 per cent of the Wash. Although the areas occupied by the reservoirs would only be used for water storage, areas between the reservoirs and the shoreline could be used for agricultural, conservation or leisure purposes. The project, however, was not carried out.

'Managed retreat' are new words in the fenman's vocabulary, and are words to rouse fenman's ancestors from their graves, men who had done battle with the

Whittlesey Wash in flood. (RS)

Managed retreat. Land reclaimed from the sea in the 1980s (left) is now reverting to saltmarsh after it was intentionally breached in 2002 to allow the sea to enter. This area is at Frieston Shore, a popular seaside resort in the nineteenth century. The nearby open prison inmates refer to this bank as 'the Bank Too Far'. (RS)

inhospitable North Sea since Roman times, and triumphed. These words describe the process of giving up land that has been reclaimed from the sea back to the sea, a process alien to the fenman and contrary to his upbringing: for him this is turning the clock back a thousand years. But it is only practised in areas where no loss of life is involved. One such area is on the northern shoreline of the Wash near Frieston: only reclaimed from the sea in 1976, this arable land will now revert to marsh – a major step back in history for the fen drainers.

But who knows what may come in the future, with topsoil disappearing at an alarming rate and increased land usage for urbanisation? Almost all the houses built in the Fens are on Grade I land around the towns and villages, this being the areas that were the driest to settle on in medieval times. This is yet another exploitation of the Fens' most fertile soils, buried under bricks and concrete, never to see the light of day again and barely sustaining any life. When soil in the Fens was under nature's control and not mankind's it did sustain life. Our modern ideals of biodiversity can only sustain life if there is a place for life to exist in, and that place is the topsoil itself. The acreage of farmed land in the Fens continuously increased from Roman times until 1979, when the last land was reclaimed from the sea; now it is rapidly decreasing, not being given back to fertile nature but returned to its first origins, when this planet sustained no life at all. One day we may have to reclaim and farm the Wash whatever the conservationists may think. The loss of valuable farmland for food production will be the driving force, unless we live on genetically modified foods. I am sure that Nathaniel Kinderley and Sir John Rennie's vision of farming the Wash back in the eighteenth and nineteenth centuries will in the long term turn out to be more than just a dream.

Many times in history events have been brought about by our succumbing to pressures or influences of the day rather than looking backwards or forward in time. Such events often occur when policies are neither thought out nor evaluated in terms of the consequences they may create. This is what happened in the Fens at a time when food was not in short supply but plentiful across most of Europe. During the late 1960s and '70s the Cowbit and Crowland Washes were drained and cultivated, funded partly by government, which had the Common Market in mind. Grain was produced surplus to the country's requirements so as to fill intervention stores funded by the taxpayer. Once more, another piece of the Fen was destined to change, not for moral or economic necessity, or even just to fulfil the fenman's passion for draining land, but because farmers were encouraged to exploit the land by 'the system', aided and encouraged by politicians, the same people who a decade or two later would curse the farmer for destroying fen, marsh, wetlands, down and hill land.

In 1870, after the draining of the Great Level and the meres, farming had to compete against world markets. This was a time when grain and meat were imported because Britain could not compete with the low production costs of the pampas and the prairies; and yet in trying to match this competition historic areas of the Fens were destroyed. Large areas of land here went into disuse at this time;

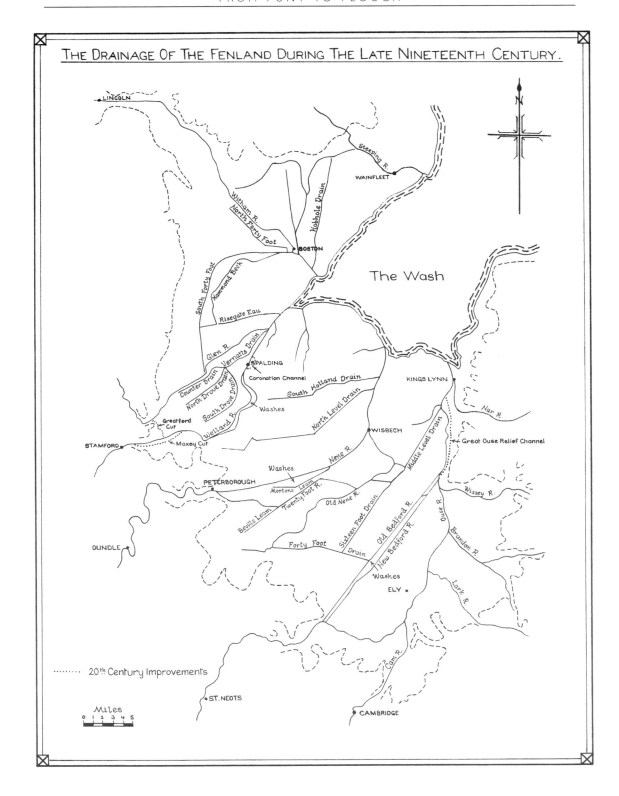

THE DRAINAGE OF THE FENLAND DURING THE LATE NINETEENTH CENTURY.

and because such land is of little value to farmers, might we witness the same scenario again in the near future with pressure from world trade organisations forcing countries to trade more freely around the globe? The mantra of politicians to appease the whim of conservation groups by turning our farmlands into fields of fauna and flora instead of crops could also influence this change. Wheat is now flooding in at prices that are sometimes lower than our own production costs from the prairies of Argentina, a country that we were at war with less than two decades ago. The year 2002 saw cheap grain enter Britain for the first time since the Crimean War from Eastern Europe, especially from the Ukraine, with some of these countries exporting grain at below their own production costs in return for hard currency. Some years ago the radioactive fall-out from the nuclear power station at Chernobyl took land out of production in parts of Europe and the higher lands of this country.

Planting potatoes on Cowbit Wash, spring 2003. The machine in the centre is working a power harrow making a seedbed, the one on the left is de-clodding the beds and the one on the right is planting the potatoes. (RS)

Two rubber-tracked tractors working land and drilling vining peas, 2002. This is part of an 11,000-acre programme for Holbeach Marsh Co-operative, who produce '90-minute peas' (from field to factory in 120 minutes for freezing). (RS)

Left: Ford Versatile 946, 330 hp tractor pulling a Dowdswell 8-furrow plough on the author's farm. (RS)

Below: A team of four FMC six-wheel pea viners between shifts, used to harvest peas for freezing. These machines work day and night during the pea season in June, July and part of August. (RS)

With such volatility in the world it is not beyond the realm of possibility that if nuclear or chemical weapons are used, large areas of land would be unusable for food production for perhaps hundreds of years to come. If farming, which is the core of the fenland economy, becomes unprofitable, might we see managed retreat around the Wash, Cowbit and Crowland Washes returned to wetlands and the reincarnation of the Fen Tiger? Or, in that precarious future, when topsoil becomes a scarce commodity in this and other countries around the globe, the Tiger may have to be buried again and pushed eastwards into the sea.

CHAPTER FOUR

'Water Loves its Own Way'

THE FENS IN LIMBO

It could be said that during the eighteenth century the Fens were in limbo, while the nineteenth century was a golden age for drainage, the age of steam power and industrial might. A good memorial to this turning-point in drainage history is the post in Holme Fen erected in 1851 on the clay beneath the peat with its top at the level of the land: it now stands 13 feet above the remaining soil, representing a kingdom gone for ever.

The 1861 General Drainage Act was followed by a wartime measure, the Land Drainage Act of 1914, which granted powers for a period of two years to the Ministry of Agriculture and Fisheries to nominate temporary commissions with limited instructions to drain land. In 1918 there followed a further Land Drainage Act, which unsuccessfully tried to carry out the excellent decision of the select

A bucket dredger cleansing a fen drain, the spoil being elevated by conveyor to the bank, 1897. (CC)

committee of the House of Lords 'to secure uniformity and completeness of action'. By 1920, 200 of the 361 drainage authorities in England and Wales had been brought into being by special Acts of Parliament but much of the fen drainage was still operating with medieval management far behind our continental neighbours. The fenland rivers from source to outfalls were under varying management bodies, often with conflicting interests and still a thorn in the side of fen drainage.

In 1927 a Royal Commission was set up to examine the workings of the drainage authorities in England and Wales. The result was a tangle of authorities, inadequate resources and conflicting ideas. This was nothing new: a select committee of the House of Lords had reported as far back as 1877 that changes needed to be made to the whole concept of water management in the Fens if they were to prosper as an agricultural area. This was recognised by some politicians, resulting in the Land Drainage Act of 1930, which saw the demise of the commissioners and the end of almost 700 years of fen tradition, the first commission having been set up by Henry III in 1258. Internal Drainage Boards (IDBs) were set up and River Catchment Boards formed, all fully represented by elected members at last dividing the management of rivers and land drainage. The Great Ouse, the Welland and Nene, and the Lincolnshire Rivers Area Authority came into being to manage the rivers traversing the Fens.

The old system of rating, which had been in force since 1532, was also to change with the 1930 Act, which stipulated that rates would now be levied using the income tax system of Schedule A and payment was related to the value of property. IDBs appointed valuers to value buildings and property at a rate in the pound of their value, as opposed to the old system of a rate per acre. This is still the basis of the rating system in use today, the only change being when in 1991 buildings used for agricultural and horticultural purposes were also included.

INTERNAL DRAINAGE BOARDS (IDBS)

Since the 1930 Land Drainage Act the 361 IDBs have functioned under their own separate administration governed by their own board members and commissions. With new modern and improved pumping systems coming on to the market and the advent of the diesel engine, larger areas of the Fens would have to be managed by fewer IDBs. The smaller boards would now have to amalgamate into larger ones enabled by the 1930 Land Drainage Act.

An example of the changes at this period can be seen with the Black Sluice. The Black Sluice commissioners had functioned as a minor catchment board up until the 1930 Act. Their duties were to maintain highland watercourses and banks in the catchment area of the rivers Witham and Steeping, an area of some 820,000 acres. The Witham and Steeping Catchment Board was constituted under the provisions of the Land Drainage Act of 1930, by the Witham and Steeping Rivers Constitution Order of 1930. They would, from now on, manage the two rivers from their source to the outfalls, leaving the management of the waters in the Fens to the newly formed Black Sluice IDB. Eighteen separate IDBs were amalgamated

Denver Sluice and Salters Lode stands at the point where five watercourses converge; the Old and New Bedford Rivers, Salters Lode, the New Cut-off Channel and the Great Ouse.

Dog in a Doublet Sluice on the River Nene at high tide with Whittlesey Wash in flood in the background. (RS)

Foul Anchor Sluice at the outfall of the North Level Main Drain into the River Nene. The Grade II listed sluice was built in 1859 by Grizzel & Co. under the guidance of George Robert Stevenson. (RS)

by the newly formed board in 1934, a daunting task in itself requiring patience and diplomacy on the part of the chairman and board. It had a catchment area of 160,000 acres of which 60,000 acres was rated, the remaining 100,000 acres being run off from the highlands on its boundaries. Their main drainage channel was the South Forty Foot Drain, an artificial drain 21 miles long cut originally in 1654. This work had been undertaken by the Earl of Lindsey and other adventurers, and is referred to in Dugdale's *History of Embanking and Draining* as 'the Lindsey Level'. The drain had indeed been improved since then but in 1934 still relied on gravity discharge at the outfall at Boston. The depression in agriculture and industry during the 1920s and 1930s, the frequent flooding in the low-lying areas of Fens and war looming in Europe made the government consider making grants available for drainage. The resulting 1937 Agricultural Act provided grants to IDBs of between 30 and 50 per cent of the cost of drainage schemes, which assisted much-needed projects to prepare agriculture to fulfil its role in the Second World War.

With war imminent in 1939, the War Agricultural Executive Committee was formed to supervise increased food production, of which improved drainage was a part. The South Forty Foot Drain and Black Sluice at the outfall were taken over by the Witham and Steeping River Catchment Board with a view to installing pumps, another main event in the Black Sluice history. This came to fruition in 1946 when major works were carried out on the internal drains as well as the South Forty Foot

A steam dredger and barges cleaning out the Sixteen Foot Drain in 1933. (LRC)

An early floating dragline cleaning the Sixteen Foot Drain and depositing the spoil on the banks, 1933. (LRC)

A Ruston Bucyrus 32 RB rope dragline owned by the Nene Navigation Co., working on the River Nene. Also seen here is a steam dredger working in the river. Rope machines such as this are still used on the rivers for mudding out. (LRC)

The Environment Agency pumping station at Boston on the South Forty Foot Drain has a pumping capacity of aprox 800,000 gallons per minute. Powered by three Ruston & Hornsby 900hp diesels and two English Electric 975hp diesels, these pumps maintain water levels for 175,000 acres.

Fortreys Hall pumps. On the left are three electric submersible pumps. The buildings have two diesels, a Ruston & Hornsby 300 hp and a British 300 hp. The tall building once housed a steam beam engine. (Sutton and Mepal IDB)

drain itself; but the icing on the cake was the installation of pumps. These consisted of 3 Ruston vertical 5-cylinder 900 hp diesel engines driving 100-inch diameter vertical pumps. They served the board well at the time but proved incapable of coping with excess water because of better land drainage and run-off. This led to the schemes of 1964, where new cuts were made, drains widened and deepened, and many internal pumps installed throughout the Board's area. To cope with this, additional pumps were installed at the outfall at a cost of almost £2 million. These pumps still operate today. Many other IDBs in the Fens went through similar re-structuring over this period, with the amalgamation of smaller IDBs, large-scale drainage works and installation of large modern pumping stations. Traditions in the Fens die hard and despite the pressure to modernise, the management of drainage has still not changed in some fen areas.

In 1965 the Ministry of Agriculture Fisheries and Food still listed 374 separate drainage districts throughout England and Wales, with 120 of these being in the Fens. Today this figure is nearer 50, with almost four-fifths of them being in the Middle Level Levels area, the last bastion of fen independence.

The 1930 Land Drainage Act brought into being the much-needed River Catchment Boards which took over the entire management of all rivers from source to outfall with rates from the local councils and special contributions from the IDBs to finance them. This system of river management was proving unsatisfactory after the Second World War, and so in 1948 the government replaced the catchment boards with river boards. So far as land drainage was concerned it had little or no effect on IDB management but did give the catchment boards responsibilities for fisheries and pollution control.

The opening of Pode Hole pumping station in 1963. Left to right: -?-, T.R. Pick OBE (chairman), Des Miles (chief engineer), the Bishop of Lincoln. (RS)

Left: The North Level IDB pumping station at Tydd was built between 1937 and 1941. During the 1947 floods these pumps operated continuously for six weeks, saving many thousands of acres of valuable farmland. Here Peter Atkins proudly surveys his machines. (RS)

The pumps at St Germans with Geoff Cave (ex-Chief Engineer of the Middle Level Commissioners) standing beside one of them. (RS)

Top left: Hobole pumping station, Witham Fourth District IDB. A man who loves his engines and pumps, David Sommerfield (pump attendant) standing alongside one of three Allen 770 hp 6-cylinder vertical two-stroke engines. Top right: Freddie Gibbon, assistant pump attendant in the 1950s beside Mirless Blackstone 250 hp diesel pump. Freddie only came in to help with the pumps in times of excessive pumping and was paid overtime, a rare occurrence. When this happened he sang: 'When it rains, it rains pennies from heaven', hence the smile! Bottom left: David Stimpson, assistant pump attendant of the Sutton & Mepal IDB pumps at Mepal standing next to a Ruston & Hornsby 300 hp diesel engine which he keeps operational in case of emergency. Bottom right: Nigel Deans, pump attendant at the Welland & Deepings IDB's Pode Hole pumps, standing beside one of three Ruston & Hornsby 650 hp diesel engines.

One of the outcomes of this change was two of the largest drainage schemes undertaken since Vermuyden's day: the Welland and the Great Ouse Flood Protection Schemes, brought about by the disastrous floods of 1947. Under the provisions of the 1963 Water Resources Act River Boards were replaced by Water Boards, which started operation in 1965. In 1974 ten regional water authorities were created to administer the sole management of water resources throughout England and Wales, the Anglian Water Authority covering an area from Humberside to the Essex coast which encompassed all of the Fens. All rivers throughout the country came under one management by the NRA between 1990–5 superseded then by The Environment Agency in 1994–5; they maintain all the main rivers that cross the Fens, some of the main drains and pumping stations in them as well as sea defences around the Wash. Their largest pumping station is at the outfall of the south Forty Foot Drain at Boston which has a capacity of pumping 8,000 gallons per minute.

The drainage of the Fens is more important today than in Vermuyden's or Rennie's day, because should a calamity occur the loss of life and revenue now would be immeasurable.

Above: A Brush 4-cylinder flat 300hp engine driving a Gynnnes Invincible Axial pump at the Sutton and Mepal pumping station.

Two Ruston & Hornsby diesel engines installed in 1936, and decommissioned in 1971. (Witham First IDB)

DRAINAGE AUTHORITIES TODAY

The Environment Agency is responsible for all the upland rivers that run into the Fens as well as the South Forty Foot Drain. The Middle Level Commission rose out of the ashes of Bedford Level Corporation in 1920, and covers land mainly in the southern section of the Fens. The Commission oversees thirty-five IDBs and drainage districts, with a catchment area of 170,000 acres of which most are below sea level. Using 113 pumping stations, all the land is pumped once, 80 per cent of it twice and 20 per cent three times.

The King's Lynn Consortium was created in 1965. Now made up of sixteen IDBs, initially there were six, in north and west Norfolk. They manage 160,000 acres in the eastern section of the Fens and 90,000 acres spread across Norfolk to the coast as far as Great Yarmouth. This was the first time in history a joint management consortium was formed by boards either in or outside the Fens.

The Witham Forth IDB has a catchment area of just over 100,000 acres in the northern section of the Fens north of the River Witham. This board also has much low-lying land, of which all is pumped once and some twice. It consists of varying types of soils from black fen to some of the most valuable silt soils in the UK between Boston and Skegness. Some silt land recently made over £12,000 per acre.

The Great Ouse Branch and the Ely Group of IDBs, with a catchment area of 112,000 acres, manages fen and upland, which at one time was part of the South Level Commissioners, who like the Middle Level Commissioners and the North Level, began its life after the demise of the Bedford Level Corporation. This area is in the southern section of the Fens with the upland being south of the New Bedford River.

The North Level IDB broke away from the Bedford Corporation in 1857 after negotiations lasting four years. It was the Duke of Bedford who had the Thorney estate, the Earl of Lincoln, as well as other owners of land in the North Level including the manor of Crowland (Lord Burghley) who joined forces to break away. The NL IDB has a catchment area of 72,000 acres in the central section of the Fens consisting of a variety of silts, black land and heavy soils, all pumped once with around 8,000 acres pumped twice.

The South Holland IDB's catchment area of 96,000 acres is between the North Level and the Wash. In 1974 five separate boards in the South Holland area were reconstituted to form the SH IDB. The board's area is much higher than many others in the Fens and consequently it is the only one that does not pump its main watercourse, the South Holland Main Drain, but discharges into the River Nene near Sutton Bridge by gravity discharge with the tides. To illustrate how drainage has changed over the past thirty years it is interesting to note that before 1968 there were only three pumps draining 15,000 acres operated by the board, out of the total 95,000 acres. Today virtually all the land is pumped, mainly owing to the increase in urbanisation in this area over the past thirty years: it is often not realised that IDBs have to drain roads, villages, towns and industrial developments as well as farmland. A new pumping station was opened this year in Holbeach Marsh at Lawyers Sluice. The sluice had previously operated by gravity discharge into the Wash but was now operating efficiently with the assistance of the pumps (which were named after one of its late vice-chairmen, Mr Stuart Hay, a well-respected farmer and drainer who farmed nearby).

The Welland and Deepings IDB was formed under the chairmanship of T.R. Pick OBE in 1972, and is made up of five separate boards. The area drained is 107,000 acres consisting of all soil types and like many other IDBs the lowest land to be drained is the farthest away from the outfalls. This board has never lacked vision both on installing new pumping stations in the past and the ability to combine drainage in the present day with conservation for the future.

The engineer's role is always changing; in the past his main task was to relieve the Fens of water as quickly as possible. Internal Drainage Board engineers today have always to be on their guard against a deluge of rain. When this happens several factors come into play. The high country drains and rivers that run through the Fens can be full to capacity with water from outside their catchment areas, yet these are the rivers that many of the IDBs need to discharge their water into. High tides can also play an important part when discharging water into the sea especially when the winds are blowing from a north-easterly direction. These two factors alone can have a devastating effect on the flow of the rivers into the Wash which the engineers are always on the lookout for. When it happens it is always of great concern to them.

Almost all the Fens are under-drained, with either clay or plastic pipes overfilled with porous filling, although the dykes and drains they run into are in far better condition now than in the past. Houses have been built in the Fens at a phenomenal rate over the last thirty years. All these factors increase surface run-off, adding pressure on the engineers, who must therefore have an eye for detail, an air of conviction and never trust to luck – for sometimes luck runs out. They, like their predecessors, need vision, the courage of their convictions and the ability to see their work completed. The drainage systems we have today have evolved through the ingenuity of innovative engineers; but we must never forget this would not have been possible without local knowledge.

Many discoveries about the past have been preserved under layers of soil many feet below the surface, not only relating to our past human existence but about weather patterns and natural catastrophes, which of course, in turn, have affected life in the Fens. I am sure that in the bowels of the Fens there are many more exciting discoveries of our fenland past lying waiting to be discovered. If freak weather patterns caused catastrophes in the past, it is not beyond the bounds of possibility that it could happen again. Should we ask the question that if they did occur again could our modern systems cope, if so all is well, if not what would need to be done to cope? It is a daunting thought, well beyond the minds and courage of politicians and the Environment Agency. If such a calamity were possible would we pander to the words 'managed retreat' or would we look for a twenty-first-century Vermuyden? This is a difficult question but one that may have to be resolved one day in the future.

THE DANGER BELL

Improvements to Fenland drainage systems will never cease. Many new drains were cut and others improved in the twentieth century, and the work continues today. The subject of fen drainage and flood protection comes naturally to fen people, especially to farmers – it's almost a sixth sense, an obsession to harness the elements and never to concede to nature's affront. Farmers cannot crop the soils without drainage any more than the urban population the Fens sustains today could live without it. For many of those that work with drainage it is more than a job and an interest, it is a passion, and indeed to some it is an ancient fen cult. Fen people remember the dry and wet seasons, the freak storms and the severe frosts going back hundreds of years. Dates are embedded in the annals of their mind as part of their genealogy, reminders of what nature has done, and can do again. 'Those who ignore the past and stumble through the present, are fated to be players in the wrong kind of future', and that future is the very survival of the Fens themselves.

As long as run-off increases, with mankind increasing his living, working and leisure space, systems will always needed to provide future improvements.

No less than sixty-two pumping stations were erected during the Second World War at a cost of £416,000, improving an area of 283,000 acres, and grants were made available to under-drain agricultural land with tile drains. Machines were developed to lay porous tiles instead of laboriously by hand, an example being the Bucheye tile draining machines from the USA which were owned and contracted out by the War Agricultural Executive Committee. Since the last war there have been major improvements made to many of the drainage systems across the entire Fens. The demand for food during the two world wars brought more land into cultivation, leading to the need for better drainage; however, this increased the shrinkage of the black Fens.

The twentieth century was certainly the century of pumping systems, diesel and electric powered, of phenomenal outputs. I would say that a pumping station such as that at St Germans has more output than all the pumping stations in the entire Fens in the year 1900. It is a pity we do not have these facts from so little time ago, for this shows how much of the history of this part of England has been lost. In the South Level up to the 1950s large-scale flooding still occurred after abnormal storms. This was due to water from the highland rivers running into the east of the Fens and so into the Great Ouse river. This area had been always been a problem since the commencement of draining the Fens – indeed Vermuyden had the answer to this in the seventeenth century – but his plans were considered too ambitious at the time. The Great Ouse River Catchment Board in 1940 called in Sir Murdoch MacDonald & Partners to advise and prepare a scheme to solve this age-old problem, but once again the plans were turned down, deemed too expensive at the time. Their plans were eventually carried out on an even larger scale after major flooding in 1947 and the 1950s by cutting a drain from Mildenhall linking up the rivers Lark, Nettle, Ouse, and Wissey, known as 'The Great Ouse Flood Protection

Wiggenhall St Germans, the largest pumping station in the Fens, was built in 1934 and owned by the Middle Level Commissioners. It has a capacity of 5,000 tonnes per minute (over 1 million gallons per minute). (RS)

Scheme' between 1954 and 1964. It then joined with the Hundred Foot Drain and carried on up to Barton Mills parallel to the Great Ouse, solving the age-old problem of highland water running into the Fens. It is called 'The Cut Off Channel', not a name I might add worthy of the engineer who designed it, or indeed the ancient route it crosses, 'Hereward Way'.

TESTING THE FEN MEN: THE 1947 FLOODS

In the 1930s engineers involved in the River Catchment Boards, Internal Drainage Boards and Drainage Commissions associated with water management in the Fens realised that improvements were needed to cope with the possibility of flooding as a result of extreme weather conditions. An area singled out as being particularly vulnerable was the southern section of the Fens – an area Vermuyden and Rennie had also identified as a potential 'disaster area' because of the familiar problem of highland run-off from rivers such as the Cam. Another area that realised, rightly, that it would suffer under freak weather patterns was the area along the River Welland.

Despite these realisations and a certain amount of planning, the outbreak of the Second World War postponed these much-needed works. The War Agricultural Executive Committee was formed to supervise the increase of home-produced food, with no less than sixty-two pumping stations erected at a cost of almost £500,000 improving an area of 283,000 acres. This has the effect, as well as improving land for farming, much of which had been under grassland, of increasing surface run-off and the pressure on the rivers running into and across the Fens.

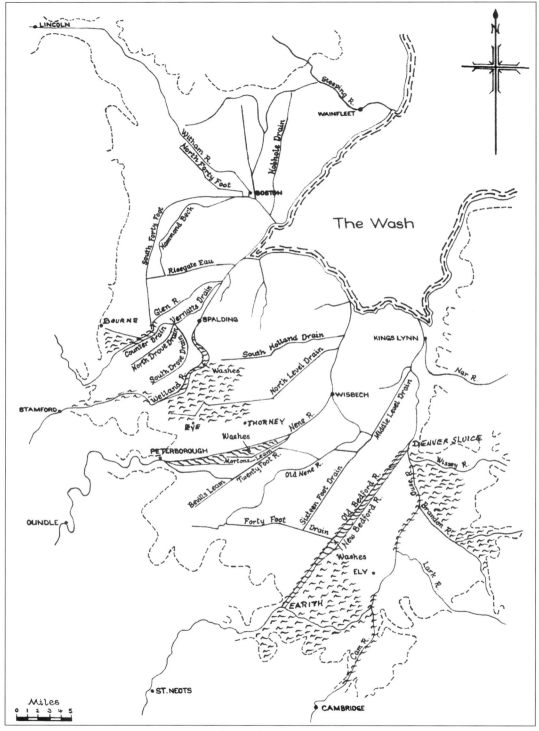

The main areas that suffered during the 1947 floods.

At the end of the war food was still in short supply, and much of it rationed. The climate was not propitious, however, for maximum yields. In 1946 the annual rainfall in the Fens was 27.19 inches, 5 to 6 inches above average, with almost 10 inches falling in October, November and December. The year 1947 also began with severe weather conditions, with snowdrifts of 20 feet in some areas in February, followed by almost arctic frosts. Many areas of the country were without electricity and the RAF was called in to drop food supplies to isolated villages, some of which had been cut off for two weeks. Wheat stocks in the country were, according to a government spokesman, 'uncomfortably low', which meant that beer production had to be cut by half and meat and bread rations reduced. The Fens was one of the country's major food producers, especially of potatoes, and the haulage strike of this year brought added problems in terms of distribution, which led to potato rationing. By the end of February 1947 the Fens, but more importantly its catchment area of over 4 million acres, were covered in deep snow and its watercourses frozen with thick ice, the equivalent of about 6 to 8 inches of rain that would have to be vectored in to the Wash in a short space of time. The stage was set for one of the greatest and most costly inundations in the history of the Fens at a time of the nation's greatest need for food.

Flood water passing under a bridge, 1947. (CC)

A flooded farmstead and farmland in the southern fens during the 1947 floods. (CC)

People watching floodwater pour through a breach after battling to contain it under extreme conditions in 1947. (Harvest Home)

The breached bank. (Harvest Home)

And sure enough, mother nature did choose to test the fen men to their limits and try to reclaim the great meres she had lost to him centuries ago. On Monday 10 March a thaw set in melting the snow, which quickly turned into torrents of water running into the fen rivers from the high country, and added to this heavy downpours of rain and more snow filled frozen drains to capacity. Vermuyden's washes between the Bedford rivers, along the Nene and Welland, were already covered in water and ice. By Thursday 13 March water from the Cottenham Lode was overflowing into the Fen and water had risen 8 feet in the Eastern fen area. Engineers were already concerned and orders were sent out on the morning of 14 March 'to stand by the banks, and all rivers to be patrolled'. Pumping stations across the whole of the Fens could not pump the water efficiently because of huge lumps of ice that were restricting the flow of water. In the eastern and southern areas, from King's Lynn to Ely and along the rivers running from the eastern high ground, especially the Lark, on Saturday water was spilling over the banks and minor slips occurring in many places.

By Sunday everyone was on full alert and emergency plans were put into place after southerly winds at gale force began to whip the water into sizeable waves that dashed against the sagging banks, causing severe damage. At around 4 p.m. the wind, at almost hurricane force, veered to the south-west – the worst possible direction for the floods a drainage engineer could wish for. Mother nature was

Planning the battle in an operations room in the southern section of the Fens, 1947. (CC)

Sometimes only a few hours' notice was given for people to evacuate farms and salvage possessions, 1947. (CC)

Barges being loaded with material to fill a breach. (CC)

testing the fenman's ability to control water far beyond anything he had experienced before. But up to this point he was holding his own against her. All able-bodied hands, drainage workers, farm workers, prisoners of war and volunteers were either at work on the banks or on standby, and an operations room was set up at Ely. Minor breaches were occurring on the River Lark and along the Great Ouse between Earith and Over where people were already moving livestock, vehicles and any other chattels they could on to higher ground. Water was still rising with winds so strong that men working on the banks could hardly stand up and communicate with each other. Soaked to the skin, tired and realising that they could not hold the banks much longer they finally yielded to the elements with the first major breach occurring on the Little Ouse, which brought flooding at Lakenheath and Feltwell fens on Sunday, at around 9 p.m.

Another serious breach occurred on Monday on a stretch of the Great Ouse, known as the Ely Ouse, at Little Thetford, flooding 2,000 acres of Thetford and Stretham fens. The government had by this time realised the massive logistical problems the operations were experiencing and drafted troops in to assist the fen people. Communications had been almost impossible across the Fens and supplies of equipment and food were desperately needed at a time of crisis to the nation's food supply.

The most serious breach of all occurred on the Great Ouse at Over Fen on Monday, and by Tuesday thousands of acres were flooded east from Earith across to the River Cam. Just as serious were the problems at Welland around Cowbit and the Crowland Washes. Bringing water from its catchment area in Lincolnshire and Leicestershire the Welland had already filled these flood washes that had frozen and provided some of the best skating for several years. When the thaw set in they filled to bursting point and with the high winds and large pieces of ice breaking up slips

Even the good Lord could not stop the floodwaters, 1947. (CC)

The last straw – chickens and haystacks marooned during the floods. (CC)

The breach at Crowland in 1947. The breach was infilled with Neptune troop carriers which floated out when the floodwater was pumped back into the Wash. (Harvest Home)

Youngsters standing in the flood water, 1947. (CC)

in the banks occurred in several places. The banks around the washes were the responsibility of two authorities, the Welland Catchment Board on the north and the North Level Commissioners on the east, and by Friday 14 March both authorities were concerned for the safety of fens either side the washes. As elsewhere, all able-bodied men filled sandbags and repaired minor breaches in the banks. The town of Spalding, already known to be a bottleneck for water passing down the Welland, had another problem, that of large lumps of ice that had broken up in the washes and were piling up in front of the bridges, thereby restricting the flow of water. Men were employed to stand on the bridges day and night breaking these lumps of ice with poles to try to increase the flow of water through the town. Ice was also being blown against the barrier banks along the east side of the washes causing slips and weakening the banks themselves. Under appalling conditions the fenmen were convinced they would avert disaster, but mother nature would beat them in the end. On Friday 21 March, three days after the main breaches had occurred, disaster struck in the western side of the Fens. Water had penetrated the bottom of the bank on the North Level Commissioners side and was undermining it so that it could hold no longer. At midday words echoed from one of the men on the bank 'She's gone! She's gone!' The washes had been breached for the first time since Vermuyden had built them in the seventeenth century. Water poured through the breach now 180 feet wide, forming a tidal wave 20 feet high which raced across Postland and Morris Fen as far as the villages of Thorney and Eye, covering valuable farm land. A worker had raced to Crowland to warn them the bank would burst with instructions to sound the air-raid siren but there was no electricity to power it. The abbey came to the rescue and the ancient danger bell was rung for the first time since the great flood of 1880.

Operations centres were established complete with workshops, field kitchens and communications to direct operations. (CC)

With telephone lines down army dispatch riders were used to keep the communications open. Railways were used to ferry men and supplies to the front line. (CC)

A breach being filled with Neptune troop carriers. (Harvest Home)

A wall of sandbags had been built the previous night along the road I lived on to form a barrier in case a breach occurred on the east side of Cowbit Wash. The work was carried out by troops who used our farmyard as a centre for supplies and a food kitchen, work that proved its worth. I had been evacuated to Cowbit from the farm and watched Cowbit Wash empty quickly not knowing where the breach had occurred, wondering if our farm was flooded. When the bank was breached it flooded land to within a few yards of our house, but the wall prevented the floodwaters spilling north into the Cowbit and Spalding area. One family in Postland refused to evacuate their house but the morning after the floods came a white sheet was seen hanging from the bedroom window. An amphibious vehicle was dispatched that day to rescue them.

Not all areas of the Fens suffered flooding, however. The River Witham held its banks, with no flooding of any consequence. The rivers Wissey and Lark averted breaching by sheer hard graft and determination by its work force and the River Nene together with its flood relief reservoir Whittlesey Wash won the day with no flooding in its area. The North Levels Tydd pumping station drew much of the floodwaters that had escaped from the Crowland wash and pumped continuously for six weeks.

Massive pumps were brought in from far afield after the breaches had been filled in, to pump the water back into the washes and rivers. (Harvest Home)

The flooding in many areas, especially the Welland breach, was contained by some of the medieval banks and railway embankments linked up by sand bag walls. This work often carried out at extremely short notice would not have been possible without local knowledge in a land where a fenman will call a piece of soil 10 feet above sea level a hill. Many lessons were learnt from this disaster with the result that many of the plans previously drawn up in case of disaster were now carried out. It may also have contributed to the replacement of the various River Catchment Boards with the River Boards in 1948.

The government was ever-mindful of the situation in the Fens. The Minister of Agriculture, Tom Williams, visited the Fens to assess the damage. The government's orders were to repair the breaches, pump the floodwaters off the farmland back into the flood washes in readiness for the coming spring. With food so desperately short and much lost in the floods themselves it realised that if this land did not produce a crop for the forthcoming harvest it may well find starving people on its hands. In the Great Ouse area 45,000 acres of fen was under water and 20,000 acres in the area affected by the River Welland. W.S. Smith OBE, chairman of the North Level Commissioners, told Mr Williams during his visit it was estimated with spring approaching that if the water could be pumped off the Fen and back into the washes and rivers immediately two-thirds of the land could be sown with spring cropping to yield a harvest for 1947.

Cabbages grown on fen land after the 1947 floods fed the hungry postwar population. (Harvest Home)

Through the fenman's tenacity, fine crops of sugar beet (left) and potatoes (right) were produced on land that was flooded five months earlier. (Harvest Home)

With this as a target thousands of pumps from the Royal Navy, the fire-fighting services and even from Holland were brought in to pump the water back into the washes. A thousand troops, together with heavy equipment, field kitchens, dispatch riders and field radios were brought in to repair the damage in the Crowland area and along the Great Ouse where three more breaches had occurred. Tugs with barges were on hand, light-gauge railway tracks were laid and Neptune amphibious troop carriers were brought in to fill the breaches. On the whole this was done successfully but some three weeks after the disaster three of the Neptunes broke away and floated out of the breach allowing water to flood some of the land a second time. The operation was code-named 'Operation Neptune' and was an extraordinary triumph for those involved after such a disaster, with almost all the flooded land being sown with crops that spring.

During the 1947 floods fenmen and Second World War POWs joined forces to fight a common enemy. (Harvest Home)

Once again in our history, troops, prisoners of war and outsiders had worked side by side with fenmen to preserve their precious land, many far beyond the call of duty. Miles of sandbag walls had been built to contain the floods, breaches stemmed, pumps brought in, and the back-up necessary to service this workforce and machines. Bulldozers, draglines, lorries and other equipment were rushed in from all parts of the country, as were soldiers from a variety of regiments, many of whom had seen active service against the Germans and were now fighting mother nature. The 1947 floods will always be remembered as the time nature reclaimed a part of the Fens for a brief period; and every fenman knows she will try again sometime.

CHAPTER FIVE
'Many Worlds More'

THE FENS' UNIQUE CHARM

In his inaugural address given at the opening of the Wisbech Industrial and Fine Art Exhibition on 7 May 1866, the Revd H. Goodwin (Dean of Ely, later Bishop of Carlisle) said:

> I think that it should be borne in mind that a flat country is not without its advantages, even in respect of beautiful objects upon which the eye can rest with pleasure, and by which the artist's eye can be educated. The effects of sunrise and sunset and indeed all beauties depending upon the atmosphere, are seen nowhere better than in a district like this; everyone must have been struck occasionally with the grand cloud pictures which may be seen in a country having a wide horizon; eccentric forms, Alpine snowy ranges, weasels and whales, and every variety of hue.

Or as Charles Kingsley wrote in *Hereward the Wake*:

> Overhead the arch of Heaven spread more ample than elsewhere, as over the open sea; and that vastness gave, and still give such cloud-lands, such sunrises, sunsets, as can be seen nowhere else within these isles.

I will try to give my own evaluation. The Fens is a country of space, a place where two-thirds of your field of vision is the sky. For those that live and work in the fenlands the sky plays a great part in their landscape. There is no defining line

A fen blow in 2002 at Prickwillow. Topsoil and cropping are blown away in gale force winds, usually in the equinox periods. (Chris Jakes)

A fen blow in Connington Fen. (Neville Bailey)

between land and sky; they blend together to create a kingdom that is for ever changing. Cumulus clouds resemble hills and mountain ranges in the distance tipped with peaks covered with snow and screed. In the spring and summer the spirits of the Fens dance in the vast expanses of corn, orchestrated by the wind, reminding us of when this great fen and mere was osier and reed. They are its soul, our link with the past; we may have witnessed the destruction of the oaks, the meres and the Fen Tigers, but their spirits live on, and they are only resting for another age. Sometimes in the spring when the winds are blowing at great force and much of the black fen is void of cropping, the soil blows, causing great dust clouds that are as black as night. They fill the dykes and any other crevices they can find with these fine particles of soil, giving the appearance of the Khamsin in the deserts of Northern Africa. They are indeed an awesome sight and distressing to the farmers involved who watched their precious soil disappear before their very eyes. Are they an act of God? Some would say they are, but others say they are the fen spirits' revenge for taking away his moors and meres, living ghosts dancing to the tune of the devil.

To see an azure, cloudless sky encasing the Fens clears the mind of suburbia, pace and time, and for a moment gives you a feeling of utopia, reminding you of nature's power of counselling man. This is a time to stop time and put life into perspective, ponder for a moment why we are on this earth, and for what purpose, if any; a time to look at what we have and appreciate it, not what we want or what we demand. Many people in Lincolnshire and especially the Fens have a passion for flying. I believe it is not just the thrill of flying but a love of the sky, knowing it is so much a part of our life and a feeling to become a part of it. Shadows are created when the sun rises and departs unhurriedly, sedately and in his own good time, a reminder of his importance to this planet, a time when dawn and dusk are conducted to glorify him. His beauty is exemplified by this phenomenon, when these long shadows stretch across this flat land almost to the horizon, creating a filigree of silhouettes for just a few moments in the day. Often we see the sun and the moon on the earth's stage together, appearing in the sky at the same time, a meeting place for two old friends who never meet and whose intermediary is our earth. Weather fronts crossing the Fens at dawn and dusk are awe-inspiring, cirrus entwining with cirrus-stratus, cumulus turning sometimes into cumulo-nimbus, all glorified by colours of blues, golds, greys and ambers blended together by nature's palette. It is a harmony of colours that holds even a fenman in awe.

ABOVE THE CLOUDS

And can this be my own world?
'Tis all gold and snow,
Save where the scarlet waves are hurled
Down yon gulf below?
'Tis thy world, 'tis my world,
City, mead, and shore
For he that hath his own world
Hath many worlds more.

(Jean Ingelow, born in Boston)

MORNING

Morning is the beginning of another day and life itself is a series of beginnings. Whatever the previous happenings of the day or night before I always love to experience the sun coming up over the Fens. He is oblivious to our emotional and spiritual world only, there to sustain life itself, and yet it stirs one's passions and emotions to face the day ahead. There is a time, especially in flat terrain when for a brief moment it is semi-light before the sun appears, a very special time to experience and savour. It is a breath in time, the transition from darkness into light, when it is neither night nor day. It cannot be expressed in minutes or seconds nor seasons or situations, it is timeless and ageless and indefinable, it is when time stops and the world pauses for a brief moment. In the African bush the Zulu has a saying which in English means 'Dawn is when a man can see the horns on his cattle', an expression that could have been used here in the Fens 500 years ago, but not now, for cattle and drovers are long gone.

NIGHT

When darkness arrives on a cloudless night, this featureless flat land void of hills and mounds allows the night sky to embrace the soil and water, the stars appear encasing one in a planetarium that has no equal in the land. It is as if the night sky possesses the fen, keeping her for herself until dawn, then releasing her to the world. Our semi-light pollution-free country exemplifies its remoteness, but how long for? Hundreds of street lamps along miles of remote fen roads where no pedestrians walk, powered by fossil fuels, which pollute our night skies just to please some planner or councillor's ego. Artificial glows in the night sky where villages once stood but have now become small towns linked by ribbon developments catch one's eye when trying to look up into the night. This all helps to distract us from the Plough or Orion appearing from the equator in the east after displaying himself to the Southern Hemisphere. These are the same skies and moon that wildfowlers hunted for ducks and geese under them on the marshes, when the moon illuminated his quarry and the clouds scurrying past it indicated their speed. Harvest moon, hunter's moon, new and full moon made up his calendar of seasons. Mallard and teal, widgeon and tufted duck flighting into ponds and drains, chattering as they do so. Plovers in full flight screeching on a full moon and geese gaggling their way to their winter feeding grounds are a fenman's opera. Nature's night sounds are still to be heard, fainter than they were perhaps but still there, genes passed down for thousands of years, the same blood-lines kept alive for better times maybe?

THE ORIGIN OF THE FEN TIGER

Wheeler says that 'people were known to have settled in this part of Britain from Northern Europe called the Iceni, from the word Ychen, meaning oxen'. There was another tribe in this part of the Fens called Coritani, derived from *Cor* meaning sheep, and so they were together known as the Cor-Iceni living here before the Roman occupation of Britain. They were hunter-gatherers not practising tillage but surviving on the Fens' rich living and grazing their cattle and sheep between the marshes and the surrounding high country. Caesar's account of Britain, however, states that 'the Fen coast was peopled by Belgae, drawn thither by the love of war and plunder who had emigrated here with the Gauls only a few years before Caesar's invasion'. He considered them the most warlike of all the Gauls and defeated them in 57 BC, but remnants of their tribe continued to harass him from the south-east of Britain where they had settled in earlier years. As we have seen above, after the Romans came the Angles from northern Europe accompanied by the Saxons and Jutes.

In the nineteenth century Macaulay, in his *History of the Fens*, referred to the fen people as Fen Slodgers, describing them as a half-savage people, leading an amphibious life, sometimes rowing, sometimes wading from one firm mound to another, and known as 'Breedlings'. These people lived in raised huts scattered across the Fens and marsh on the higher ground, eking out an existence by fishing and wild-fowling in the many lakes and meres. They were said to be hard, uncouth and not friendly to others, especially outsiders and upland men whom they viewed with suspicion, wary of any attempt to change the Fens and the way of life it gave them.

James Tidswell posing in his punt on Cowbit Wash, c. 1890.

Mr Scrimshaw with his greyhound, early twentieth century when hare coursing was a popular sport. An abundance of hares and flat stone-free country around the Wash made it some of the finest running grounds in the kingdom.

Wisbech cattle market showing pens of fat cattle: thousands of cattle are fattened in the Fens on products from the farms and food-processing factories. (LRC)

The town ratcatcher in Wisbech after a good day's work in the 1930s. (LRC)

James Tidswell and his father in Cowbit Wash with punt and gun, c. 1895.

James Tidswell in Cowbit Wash holding a hammer gun and mallard, c. 1895.

Charlie Scholes with a brace of swans on Cowbit Wash, c. 1908.

Harold Pearson in 1940. He was one of the last gunners in Cowbit Wash.

James Tidswell in Cowbit Wash holding a shotgun with his punt and punt gun, c. 1888.

Below: Charlie Scholes in Cowbit Wash with his punt gun mounted on an ice sledge with a brace of swans at the front, c. 1908.

Mark Decamps on Cowbit Wash in his punt, c. 1895.

Charlie Scholes and Henry Atkin on Cowbit Wash unloading the punt of wildfowl, c. 1895.

So what was the origin of the Fen Tiger? Was he from the Belgae? I do not believe so, for he was never a warmongering soul, preferring the simple secluded life of living in and off the Fens.

Was he a fusion of Roman, Saxon, Danish and Flemish origin? Or was he the descendant of an indigenous race of people unique to the Fens conceived after the Ice Age? Some say the name Tiger has Celtic origins, and is derived from the Celtic word *Tiak*, meaning ploughman. Whatever his origins his home was his beloved fen which provided for all his worldly needs, salt and grain, fish and fuel, fowl, food and water, the essentials of life – the Fens even provided remedies for its ills such as ague (malaria) by endowing them with opium.

This was indeed utopia for the Fen Tigers. They understood that their promised land was not to be interfered with; but when their way of life was threatened they would die to maintain their birthright. In *Hereward the Wake* Charles Kingsley says that highlanders and lowlanders at some time in their history achieve greatness. There was such a period for the men of the eastern and central counties, for they proved it by their deeds. When the men of Wessex fell at Hastings once and for all, and struck no second blow, then the men of the Danelaw disdained to yield to the Norman invaders. In 1070 Hereward the Wake and his fenmen challenged the hand of God when they plundered the abbey of Peterborough in defiance of William I and his appointing a foreign abbot of Norman breeding. Kingsley writes:

For seven long years they held their own against the Normans like true Englishmen, not knowing when they were beaten until there were none left to fight. Their bones lay white on every island in the Fens; their corpses rotted on gallows beneath every Norman keep; their few survivors crawled into monasteries, with eyes picked out, hands and feet cut off; or took to the wild wood as strong outlaws like their successors and representatives, Robin Hood, Will Scarlet, and Little John; Adam Bell, Clym of the Cleugh, and William of Cloudeslee.

They may have been beaten but they never really bent their necks to the Norman yoke, they were indeed the last of the true English.

These were the very people who resisted William the Conqueror in their own country, conquered, yet not defeated. It was they who later resisted the Dutch drainers and their adventurers in draining the Fens from Kyme to Cowbit and Crowland to Ely. Resilient people, stubborn to the core, who accepted nature's moods and injustices, but found it hard to accept man's interference with nature. Whether or not they were an indigenous fenland tribe, they became an endangered species from the moment man commenced draining the Fens. Or was the name Fen Tiger a figment of the imagination, a hallucination, a demon in the fen people's minds caused by the effects of ague? When, in the seventh century, Saint Guthlac banished demons from the island of Crowland, converting the site to a holy place, was it really demons he saw or Fen Tigers? Whatever their origin, they, like the last great mere of Whittlesey, would finally be put to rest by modern man thanks to new machinery and political ideals.

Charlie Scholes and Henry Atkin on a frozen Cowbit Wash, c. 1895.

Charlie Scholes, c. 1895.

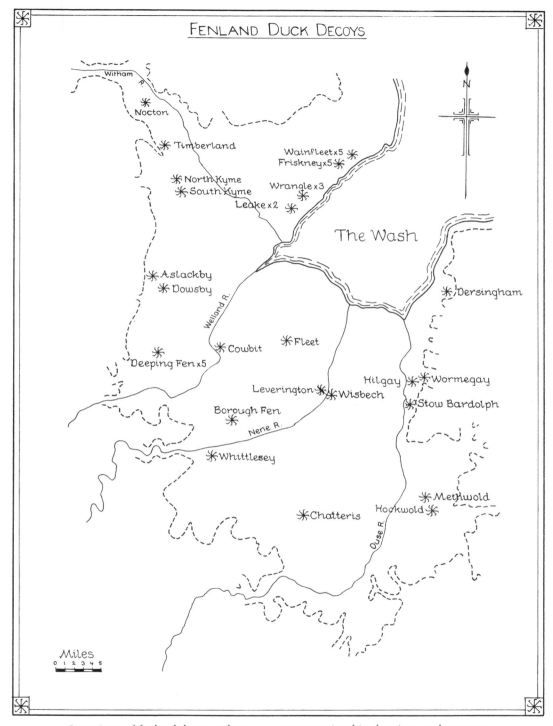

Locations of fenland decoys where one or more existed in the nineteenth century.

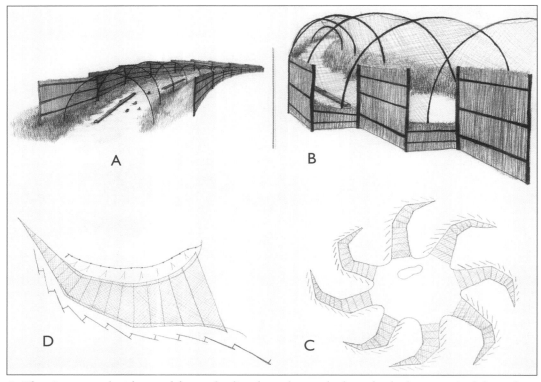

A: *The pipe covered with netted frames leading from the pond where the ducks are enticed down from the pond by the dog.*

B: *The screens and dog leaps behind which the man and dog work.*

C: *Typical decoy pond showing pipes leading off.*

D: *Diagram of pipe.*

Decoys on their stations.

A fenman, probably Bill Robinson, placing the decoy on its island, Cowbit Wash, c. 1900.

Hilkiah Burgess (1775–1868), working a decoy near Bourne, from a contemporary print.

A Simple Full Bred Fenman

Such as born in a coy and bred in a mill,
Taught water to grind, and ducks to kill;
Seeing coots clapper claw, laying flat on their backs,
Standing upright to row, and crowing of jacks;
Laying spring nets for to catch rough and reeve,
Stretched out in a boat with a shade to deceive;
Taking geese, ducks, and coots, with nets upon stakes,
Riding in a calm day for to catch moulded drakes;
Gathering eggs to the top of one's wish,
Cutting tracks in the flaggs for decoying of fish;
Seeing rudds run by shoals 'bout the side of Gill sike,
Being dreadfully venom'd by rolling in slike;
Looking hingles, and sprinks, trammles, hop-nets and teanings,
Few parsons, I think, can explain all their meanings;
In theory, no doubt, they may pretty nigh do,
But the practical part they have never gone through

Written by a fenman from Kyme Fen

Many of these occupations were to disappear when Kyme Fen was drained at the end of the eighteenth century. Gill Syke drain still exists in Holland Fen, running east from Amber Hill to the North Forty Foot drain. There are still descendants of Fen Tigers around in the Fens, not as many as there were perhaps but still there, netting eels and fishing the fen drains for course fish, especially pike. The wildfowlers shoot duck and geese in the winter and test their skill against the best flying pheasants in the land, not reared and fat but lean and fast, and who know how to fly out of range of guns. Ferreting is an old tradition used by generations of fen people to keep the rabbits down on the river and sea banks because they know what effect a hole can cause in times of flood, even today. Running dogs or long dogs to course the hare is also an ancient tradition here. The fen hares are renowned for their speed, stamina and agility – a match for any dog across the land. Sadly, this is one sport that is being abused to the detriment of the brown hare, attracting unsavoury characters from all parts of the country who seem intent on its destruction by illegal coursing.

WILDLIFE

There are still many birds to be seen in the Fens that are rare in other parts of the country. Barn owls are still common – some months ago on a summer evening I saw six when travelling a distance of 6 miles, all hunting for food for themselves and their offspring. This will change as continuing urbanisation comes to the Fens and barn conversions destroy his home. I see barn owls from my house all the year round. We live happily as neighbours and have done all my life, but sadly our friendship will end soon since the barns have been sold for conversion. They may

Plover catching (springing the net), probably by one of the Robinson family in Cowbit Wash in about 1900.

be persuaded to stay, boxes having been erected for them as a substitute for their eviction from the barn, but in the end it is they who decide where they will breed in the future, if anywhere.

Little owls are plentiful, too, while the tawnies are quite common and the long-eared found in lesser numbers in the winter months. Short-eared owls are found also in the winter months, nestling and feeding on the riverbanks among the grass, if they have not been flailed by the Environment Agency. Between the months of June 2002 and February 2003 seventy barn owls and eighteen tawny owls that had been killed on the road were taken to a local taxidermist, who is also one of the last of the Fen Tigers. The Fens probably sustains more barn owls per acre than any other part of the United Kingdom, not only because of the number of barns here but the food chain that they need.

Woodpeckers are on the increase here, as are kestrels, sparrowhawks, marsh harriers, and all predators, proving that farmers are using more environment-friendly methods of cropping and conserving the land to provide them with their food chain. Hobbies and merlin are about if you are sharp and keen enough to

Henry Atkin and Charlie Scholes about to pull the nets, Cowbit Wash, c. 1895.

James Tidswell calling the plovers into the decoys, Cowbit Wash, c. 1890.

look. The skylark has not disappeared here, having adapted to modern farming methods as many birds have done. I know, for if one thing can stir my emotions and kindle my love of this flat land it is the sound of skylarks singing their hearts out while climbing higher and higher above the Fens to sing their love song. It is the first bird to sing in the morning so you have to be 'up with the lark' to hear them. The skylark is the princess of the Fens. Plovers, for whom the moon is their calendar and their clock, call at night to remind us that the moon is full. Kingfishers flash down the drains and there is no sweeter sound than reed sedges chattering in the reedbeds enjoying life. We see many other small migrating birds passing through the fen and marsh in spring and autumn, resting and feeding here on their journey, bramling, fieldfares, wheatears. They are small to the eye but pleasing to the heart, and welcome guests in our land, a courtesy passed down from our ancestors, and will I hope passed on by future generations of fenmen.

The heron, truly the king of fen birds, still stands patiently at the sides of the drains waiting for his lunch. As they clean the fen watercourses hydraulic excavators spread the spoil on to the land alongside, often revealing small fish and eels which the heron patiently waits for. He has become the friend of the lonely drainage worker operating these machines, and is his only companion for weeks on end. Ducks, geese and Bewicks and Hooper swans are annual visitors to the Fens,

George and Bill Robinson scan the sky for birds to come to their nets on Cowbit Wash, c. 1895.

still visiting from the arctic circle as their ancestors have done since the Ice Age. Instinct has handed down to each generation of birds how to navigate their course from breeding ground to feeding ground and home – a skill it took mankind a thousand years to perfect.

We have not left much for these birds to winter on but they return to remind us it was once their land. I feel jubilant when they fly overhead en route to Welney Wash for their winter holiday, but sad and remorseful when they leave in April. It is a wonderful sight to see a flock of Bewicks in tight formation, their course set for the Tundra with 2,000 miles of hard flying in front of them. They are just starting their long journey, and it is interesting to watch the odd straggler lagging behind and calling out, not yet confident in his flying skills, but the group adjusts its formation, turning to allow him to join them and slot in: they fly in family groups and so the bond in flight is maternal. The sound of their calling to each other – or is it saying goodbye until next year? – is moving, or is it my fen ancestors reminding me of what we once had? We should look at these sights that have appeared for thousands of years and learn what we as a human race have lost.

THE EEL (*ANGUILLA*)

The importance of the eel in the Fens not only as a rich source of food but also as a trading commodity is underestimated. Unlike most freshwater fish the eel, and especially the silvers, can be kept alive in tanks or artificial ponds for months

Eel fishing with an eel glaive or stang in a fen drain. (CC)

Mick Bramwell, probably the last full-time eel fisherman in the Fens, showing one of his many fyke nets for catching eels, all of which he makes himself. (RS)

without losing condition. This makes it suitable for transporting long distances out of the Fens overland or in boats. With the availability of salt from the Fens they can be salted, cured and smoked, and provide a very high protein source of food. Before nets were used eels were caught with the willow eel trap (hives and grigs), made from willows grown over the entire Fens, and eel spears known as glaives and stangs. These spears were made by local blacksmiths to their own design, often from hardened carriage springs, and came in many shapes and sizes. Another effective and deadly method was the bab, a willow rod with line attached and a cluster of worms tied to a small bunch of worsted at the other end. This was then lowered to the bottom of the river or drain and would be eagerly taken by the eels who would not release it even when pulled out of the water. The fike net was introduced from Holland in the nineteenth century, and for commercial eel catchers this became their only tool in the rivers and estuaries.

Eels had been an important commodity in the Fens since at least the Middle Ages. Some 60,000 eels were caught in one year by twenty fishermen of Ramsey Abbey and, as we have seen, the stone used to build the abbey at Ely bought from the abbey of Peterborough was paid in sticks of eels. Of all the Fen Tigers, the eel catcher's life has changed the least over the centuries, and his work is as clandestine as it always has been. He lives not by time but by the tides and the phases of the moon. His work is conducted mostly at night, especially when the moon is black

Mick and Beverley Bramwell laying fyke nets in a gravel pit in the Fens. (RS)

(new moon) on the first run of the silvers, usually in September and again in the autumn months of October and November This is the time the silver eels migrate back to the Sargasso Sea off New Mexico. The eels' life cycle has not changed since the splitting of the continents when they were moved over to America from their European homeland 80 million years ago. They are carried in the warm waters of the Gulf Stream across the Atlantic to the Fens, up the drains that Vermuyden cut, to their feeding grounds, or what are left of them.

Eel begin life hermaphrodites but environmental conditions influence their sex while in the Fens, where they live for anything up to ten to fifteen years as brown eels before nature unleashes the maternal instinct to return home for breeding. Before this they gorge themselves with food and their bellies turn to a blend of green and silver, fuelled up with protein to sustain their long journey home to the warm waters off New Mexico. Not only do they have the protein to live on, but their shape changes. Their heads take on a more pointed shape to assist their passage through the water – scientists call this aerodynamics, fenmen call it nature. The eels leave the fen rivers and drains and head out to sea to join their relations from Europe and the Baltic to swim the long journey home to their motherland. It is usually the male silvers, who mature earlier than the females, who tend to leave on the first run in September, the females migrating later in the autumn. The females mature to a greater weight than the males and can reach up to 8–9 lb: one female

A typical fen eel hive made from local willow.

Right: A large silver eel weighing approximately 7lb.

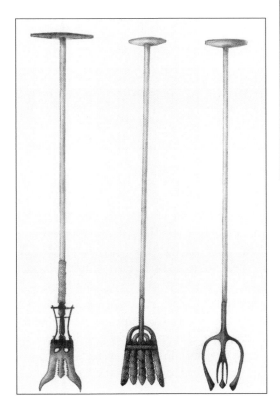

Eel glaives or stangs used to catch eels when they are in mud. In the north of the Fens they are known as stangs, derived from Old Norse sto(n)g or Dutch stang *meaning a stake or pole. The word* glaive *is derived from the Old French* glaive *meaning a sword or spear, and was probably brought over by Normans or the later settlers, the Huguenots, who settled mainly in the central part of the Fens where the word* glaive *is used.*

Silver eels transferred to a keep net after being caught in a fyke net. (RS)

I saw was about 8 lb and estimated to be well over ten years old. On reaching the Sargasso Sea the eels breed to start the lifecycle again, one of the great wonders of nature. Little is known of the eel's ecology – we know of his movements to and from the Sargasso but even there no evidence has been found of the area he actually breeds in.

The eel catcher has to be a secretive person, their activities nocturnal, away from the prying eyes of man. They still supply the London market's taste for jellied eels, while smoked eels are for the gourmet who values food more than anything on earth, and is prepared to pay for his lust, for they are an expensive delicacy. Anyone who has savoured smoked silver eel will know why the monks came to the Fens fourteen centuries ago! Most of the silvers go to Holland to please the palate of the Dutchman, who also pays for his pleasure, while the cheaper browns suit English pockets. It is difficult, or well-nigh impossible, to find records of eels caught in the Fens in the past and the eel catchers I know will not disclose their catches; even the Environment Agency, which issues licences, encounters the same secrecy. The ones I know tell me that their catches have reduced considerably over the past few years and they blame several factors, one being the lack of elvers from the sea and the restrictions by pumps and sluices of their passage up the fenland drains. Stories go around the fen that the Gulf Stream has moved its path and that the elvers are not coming to their old fattening grounds. Others say that the elvers are being caught by trawlers and used for commercial farming. Whatever the reason, one of the last full-time eel catchers I know in the Fens says that he cannot make a living catching eels now, and has found another occupation – another end to a fenland occupation that has been practised for over a thousand years. The numbers of eels caught has declined over the past few years not only in the Fens but also through Europe. Let us hope that this is just another of nature's periodical changes and that the eel does not become an endangered species. If it does, however, wish to return to the Fens in large numbers the doors have been closed to him. With the pumps and sluices we have today that restrict his passage up to the feeding grounds he will have to look for another home.

ROYAL FISH

In May 1869 a large fish was seen in Cowbit Wash opposite the village church. The fish had obviously come in with the tide along the Welland and entered the Wash, where it became stranded. The locals, realising this, dispatched the fish with a shotgun and took it to Spalding, and no doubt were paid handsomely for their catch of a 14½ stone sturgeon.

A similar event took place in 1912 when a sturgeon swam with the tide in to the River Delph at Wellmore Sluice from the Great Ouse, but as the tide started to ebb

A very proud pike angler, 1897. The Fens are renowned for large pike, one of 52lb was caught when Whittlesey Mere was drained in the 1850s. (CC)

143

the fish became stranded and could not swim out, so after much debating the locals decided that the fish had to be put out of its misery. Joey Butcher was summoned to shoot the fish with his muzzle-loading gun charged with ball bearings. The fish was dispatched to London (Billingsgate fish market), weighing in at 34 stones.

THE SHIRE HORSE

The heavy horses bred and used in the Fens were mainly the breeds of Suffolk, Clydesdale and Percheron, but the one to make his mark here was the shire. William the Conqueror introduced a type of heavy horse to Great Britain, which eventually became known as the Old English Cart Horse, with a society being formed to register the breed, the Old English Cart Horse Society. The breeders of this fine animal realised the contribution this horse was making to the economy of the country and formed the Shire Horse Society (SHS) in 1878. No doubt the name 'shire' came about because of his main breeding ground in the shire counties, four of which had land in the Fens. The shire was made for hard work, good to handle and adapted easily to this fertile land. The Fens provided food for horses that was unequalled anywhere in the land: rich grass in the summer, home-grown cereals, and the best hay that man and nature could make. Bred and fed on the fen soils and

A team of three shire horses pulling a binder, which cuts and packs the corn into sheaves, which are then stooked by hand in the field before being carted for stacking, 1930s. (LRC)

A girl leading a horse pulling a cart loaded with corn from the harvest field to the farmyard, 1930. (LRC)

the horses' by-products used to fertilise them, it epitomised the modern term 'sustainable energy'. The Fens became a breeding ground for finest heavy horses in the country not only to work here but for sale throughout the length and breadth of the country and overseas.

Until the tractor was introduced horses were used to help with cultivation and to transport crops. Indeed, as late as the 1960s many fen farms still used horses to lift potatoes. Canals had been used for centuries to transport goods but it was in the mid-nineteenth century that they reached their zenith. The barges on the canals needed strong heavy horses to propel them, so there was a huge demand for these animals from many parts of the country. The birth of the railways did take trade away from the canals and many soon became disused, but, surprisingly, this did not reduce the demand for horses – on the contrary, the demand increased with the horse being used to transport goods to and from the stations as well as for shunting trucks in the station yard. The call for the heavy horse peaked around the end of the nineteenth century, with the main buyers of horses being for the canal, the railways and the brewers. Sales of these horses at horse fairs were held regularly

A team of men and shire horses, used for pulling barges along the River Nene, Wisbech, in the late nineteenth century. (LRC)

Wisbech show, early twentieth century: a line-up of heavy horses and cattle at the grand parade. (LRC)

throughout the Fens, usually at separate locations from cattle markets. Peterborough held a horse fair up to 1952 and March held its last one in 1965. The Cole Ambrose family of Stuntney near Ely were large farmers and had an extensive breeding programme, producing up to eighty shire foals per annum for their own use when the horse was the sole power house on the farm. From 1880 to 1973 a total of 185,874 horses was registered nationally with the SHS, of which 1,989 were Stuntney horses. No other stud can even remotely approach this number: this is the most prolific stud in the history of the society.

The Shire Horse Society noted a decline in the number of shire mares registered: the figures fell from 208 registered in the early 1950s to 24 by the end of the 1960s. These figures mirrored the declining role of the working horse as a form of power across the country. A concerted effort by the society to halt the decline has been successful, supported by breeders and enthusiasts here and overseas. Much of this is due to Mr R.W. Bird MBE who took on the role of secretary of the Shire Horse Society in 1963 at a time when it could easily have ceased to exist. He not only helped to stop the decline of registrations but increased them, largely by generating support from brewers, and began to export shires to America. These two factors generated income and saved the breed.

The enthusiasm and dedication at the same time made the East of England Society showground the Mecca for heavy-horse shows, which attract people from around the world.

Heavy horses being shod, 1930s. (LRC)

SHIRE HORSE SOCIETY STUD BOOK

1898	Stallions	620	Mares	1,434
1916	Stallions	699	Mares	3,408
1941	Stallions	161	Mares	522
1953	Stallions	73	Mares	208
2002	Colts	150	Fillies	300

Of the 150 colts registered around one-third remain entire (not castrated), to be used for breeding.

A great many rough hardy horses are bred in the Fens, especially at Wildmore Fen, which are known as 'Wildmore Tits'. The carthorses now generally in use in the Fenland are strong, well-made animals, and from the mares many of the London dray horses are produced. Great encouragement has been given in recent years to the breeding of good horses by the foal fairs held annually at Boston, Donington, Holbeach and Long Sutton. There is always a good show of entire horses at the markets in the spring, £100 being paid for a good colt. A few nag horses are bred, but little attention is given to the breeding of hunters and blood horses.

It is fitting that this magnificent horse who helped to create the Fens and bring wealth to so many of its farmers, his breeders, is remembered here, with the Shire Horse Society now having its headquarters at the East of England Society headquarters at Peterborough.

INNS

Hamlets, churches, chapels and sluices are to be found down isolated droves and Fens that nestle near an inn. When drinking water was so scarce before the water mains were laid in the nineteenth century, inns played a great part in fen life, for quenching the thirst of those toiling in the fields or working in the drains.

Some of the drainage boards owned inns, and when men were working on the construction of dykes and drains they were paid with chitties to exchange for ale. Two such inns were at either end of the Vernatti's Drain, the Fishermans Arms at Pode Hole and the Ship Inn at Surfleet Seas End, both owned by the Deeping Fen IDB. They were built when the drain was cut in the seventeenth century and remained under the same ownership until they were sold off the 1950s and '60s. Many of the inns have gone, but what does remain are the drains that men who frequented these places of refreshment dug by hand, including Morton's Leam, King's Dyke, Vermuyden's Drain, the Bedford river's Lord's Drain, Pig Water, Cat Water, Fitzwilliam Drain, Pophams Eau, Lady Nunn's Old Eau, Gill Syke, Hobhole Drain, Hammond Beck, Vernatti's Drain and Canter's Doles. The names of Kindersley's Cut and Pauper's Cut have now gone, having become a part of the River Nene.

PORTS

With rivers constantly being improved over the centuries ports grew up in many places over the Fens. The Romans used Wainfleet while Bicker was used until the seventeenth century. Spalding, Fosdyke and King's Lynn were for centuries thriving ports, and Boston at one time was second only to London as the largest port in the kingdom. Sutton Bridge docks were built in 1881 but were never used, since part of the dockside collapsed before the opening ceremony; however, owing to the interest of a modern-day adventurer, Mr Peter Clery, it opened again in the 1980s and is now a thriving business. Inland towns also attracted shipping, with barges going up river to Stamford via Spalding, Lincoln via Boston and Wisbech (whose port in 1825/6 handled 1,209 ships, with 70,000 tons of cargo) along the Nene. The Great and Little Ouse were rivers of great importance, carrying river traffic to St Ives, Huntingdon and as far inland as Bedford.

Many of these ports have disappeared over time because of the coastline changes and the advent of rail and road transport into these areas. Goods are no longer transported on water but boats for leisure purposes are in great demand and there is now an intricate network of rivers and fen drains linking up to form a boating paradise. The area under the Middle Level Commissioners not only has to make sure that all of its area is drained to stop flooding but that water levels are maintained for navigational purposes, a daunting task for those involved. Shipping in and out of

A steamship on the River Nene at Wisbech in the early twentieth century. (LRC)

Timber being unloaded from steam ships in Wisbech Port. Much of this timber was used to supply the many businesses making containers for fruit and vegetables grown locally. (LRC)

the ports around the Fens has always been of small tonnage, mainly inland or European coasters, as there are no deepwater berths. When Britain joined the Common Market shipments of grains, fertilisers and other agricultural goods increased both ways and the ports of Sutton Bridge, Fosdyke, Boston, King's Lynn and Wisbech have entered this millennium as important sea links to the Fens.

OUR HERITAGE

A reasonably good outline of fen settlement and drainage can be found by looking at a modern map of the Fens. Early Anglo-Saxon and medieval settlements are indicated by smaller fields and dykes winding along small roads and old creeks, usually in the silt areas. An exception to this is Bicker Haven, south of Boston, an area of silt that was not reclaimed until the mid-seventeenth century. The areas where villages and hamlets are sparsely placed are usually the later drained areas, of the eighteenth to nineteenth centuries, where larger farms are usually found. In these areas the dykes tend to be larger and straighter, as are the roads, and at night it is even more noticeable because of the lack of lights.

The Fens still have a unique and mysterious vocabulary all of their own. Words such as droves, dykes, delphs, sluices, slackers, slipes, eaus and lodes roll easily off a fenman's tongue. Places like Clough, Cradge, Toft, and Ton are his bounty after pitting his wits, energy and resources against the elements. During our fenland history we have destroyed the past too hastily, often in the name of progress, not leaving monuments to our forebears, who were also seeking progress in their lifetimes. Drains and dykes will always remain out of necessity, but bridges, sluices, pumps and slackers of historical interest have disappeared and still are, like the fen peats. So often in our history men thought they had controlled the waters in the Fens, water from the sea, from the uplands and from the heavens, but these have been his adversaries.

Improved land drainage through field drains (pipes laid under the soil), and modern methods of farming, all assist in soil erosion. Large areas of the black fen (peat soil) are still eroding, not at the rate they did when they were first drained, but blue clay is begging to appear in many of these areas. When this happens waterlogging occurs and re-draining of the land has to be done. It is a frightening situation for a farmer to see his soil disappearing beneath him knowing that there will be little topsoil left for future generations to cultivate.

The post at Holme Fen is our reminder of this but examples can be seen in many parts of the Fens. Roads, rivers, drains and buildings are above the land where shrinkage has occurred and pumping stations have been lowered over time to cope with this problem. It is not only the black Fens that are changing, silt soils are losing their organic content through intensive farming practices forced by modern marketing and economics. Loss of organic content in the soil destroys capillary action, and this is causing waterlogging during and after heavy rainfall. Soil erosion could devastate the Fens and indeed many other parts of the world in future years – you only have to see the change in colour of our rivers and drains in the Fens after heavy rains. The water soon changes from clear to reddish brown, like the rivers often seen in Africa after rains, a sign of erosion, and topsoil being carried away to be deposited somewhere else. Governments and farming organisations have spent millions on research into

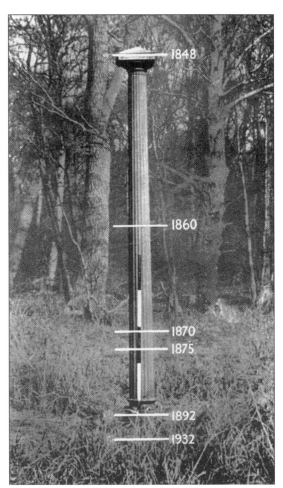

The post at Holme Fen, showing the levels of peat shrinkage since 1848. Whittlesey Mere nearby was drained in 1852.

151

improving farming techniques but little on the management and conservation of topsoils, taking them for granted.

There is nowhere in the British Isles where an area as large as the Fens has changed so much under man's imprint. Its topography is truly man-made and yet it has never lost its mystique and individual charm, which man has not been able to take away. Almost all man's modern innovations have come to the Fens, except the motorway which, up to now, has eluded them. Nothing changes countryside or its indigenous population's way of life as much as a motorway. With the arrival of the motorway an area soon ceases to be parochial and becomes a suburban annexe in which local traditions cease, accents change and local customs disappear by degrees. The world is gradually closing around us, through transportation and technology, but you can still find places in the Fens where the only sounds are those of nature.

Today many people come to the Fens to escape from modern civilisation, people who, like the Huguenots and others who sought refuge here in the past, bring new crafts and skills to the area. The rich fen soils have always grown salad and vegetable crops as well as flowers for suburbia, and now with the supermarkets' demand for packed and prepared foods massive packing stations have sprung up. This has created a demand for labour both manual and management not sustainable from local communities, which has encouraged an influx of people to the area.

THE GREAT FEN PROJECT

Nothing has ever been beyond the realms of possibility in the Fens; and in fact the great fen monster may be waking from his hibernation of one hundred and fifty years. Recently he has stirred under the auspices of the Great Fen Project (TGFP). TGFP has purchased a 205-acre farm with support from the Heritage Lottery Fund, that has increased the area of Woodwalton Reserve by 40 per cent. Near the site of the once-famous Whittlesey Mere, the reserve is in the black fen area south of Peterborough, and supports important wetland habitats, animals and plants unique to this country. Nearby is Holme Fen Reserve that contains the largest silver birch woodland in lowland Britain. Surrounded by black fen where the bog oaks appear out of the soil, this area was one of the last to be drained extensively during the mid-nineteenth century. The furthest away from the outfall, it is virtually all below sea level with most of the topsoil gone. The TGFP aims to create a wetland nature reserve across 7,500 acres of land that would join the two reserves, safeguarding and restoring some rare and threatened habitats for flora and fauna. This project could transform a large part of the Fens, attracting people for leisure, study groups and many other fields of activity associated with wetlands. We may yet see the fen man's dream come true: the restoration of some ancient hunting ground of the Fen Tiger. But one thing is certain; if the Tiger was reincarnated, modern man would destroy him immediately.

'THESE FENS ARE NOW DRAINED'

We can now say, as Vermuyden once said in the seventeenth century, 'these Fens are now drained' – or can we? Dorothy Summers in her excellent book *The Great Level* quotes Colonel William Dobson who in 1664 said 'the charge of those fenlands may not exceed the profit'. She then goes on to say, 'Today a great question mark still hangs over the Fens. Paradoxically a problem which now remains is not so much flooding as over-draining.'

This was written in 1976, an exceptionally dry year until 12 inches of rain fell during the months of August, September and October. Records can be broken, but the record of 1880 still stands, when over 14 inches fell during the months of August and October, with over 4 inches falling in four consecutive days. This caused widespread flooding across the Fens, with much loss of cropping and livestock. It was the time the Danger Bell tolled at Crowland Abbey and created much 'Bridge Talk' – when the men of Crowland congregated under the Trinity Bridge in the centre of the village and held conference on any local issue, but mostly gossip.

April 1998 saw over 6 inches of rain falling, of which over 2 inches fell on 9–10 April. The previous six months had not had above average rainfall and the averages for the previous three years were also not above the previous fifty-year average. Wheeler does not record an April with more rainfall than this but his records only go back to 1826. Most of the pumps in the Fens were at their capacity, some tested to their limits, and some had to be stopped to allow outfall pumps to catch up. There was widespread flooding along the upper catchment areas of the rivers Welland and Nene, with the main street of the village of Wansford flooded.

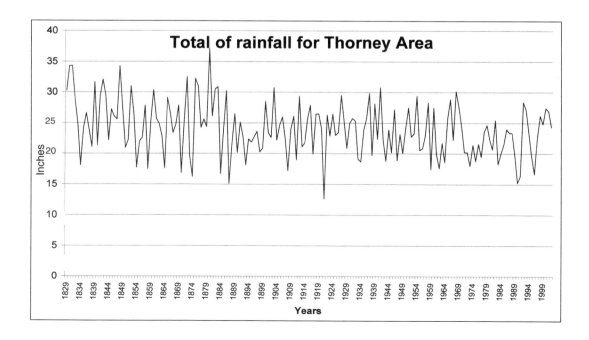

A Berkanhegar weed-cutting machine, 'The Spider', introduced from Germany in 1988. These machines are still in regular use on the Fens.

Ruston Bucyrus 30 RB rope dragline cleaning out the River Welland.

Flooding was prevented in the Fens with Whittlesey and Welney Washes full to capacity but performing as Vermuyden had designed them to do, some 350 years earlier. Georgia Sly had a herd of Belted Galloway cows and calves marooned on Whittlesey Wash for several days; they had found a high dry spot to survive on. There was a slip in the bank on the upper end of the South Forty Foot Main Drain that caused water to spill over the bank causing minor flooding; the locals say it was caused by holes made by rabbits or moles. Although we are in the age of telemetry and computers, nothing can replace the drainage worker. A rabbit, mole or rat hole in a drain bank can cause devastation when water begins to flow through them during times of flood, causing slips.

This same year Cowbit Wash almost flooded with the siphon not operating and water spilling from the Welland into the Wash itself with the risk of the bank breaking. If this had happened it would have been the first time for fifty years that the Wash had flooded, with much talk from the old men of Cowbit, saying 'I told you so'. The siphon was installed in the 1970s replacing simple stop boards on a weir, the idea being that if water in the Welland rose to a dangerous height it would set the siphon in motion to flood the Wash. This has never happened since it was installed because the necessary conditions had not prevailed until 1998. The water rose above the siphon and yet it was not set in motion, but I have it on good authority from the Environment Agency that it will work. The South Holland IDB

The siphon on Cowbit Wash showing the river level observed by local farmer Jim Ashton. (RS)

had problems when cott (an algae or blanket weed) blocked the entrances to several pumping stations, causing them not to operate to capacity. This was later overcome by installing mechanical weed screens which operate automatically, clearing the weed while the pumps are in operation. With the word conservation at the forefront of drainage today engineers are pressurised to maintain higher water levels during the summer months not only for conservation but also for the increasing leisure use of the waterways. This is correct if we have the systems in place to remove excess water after severe storms, which frequently happen during the summer months. I noticed in April 1998 that summer levels were being maintained earlier that month in some areas. We had experienced three exceptionally dry Aprils, in 1989, 1990 and 1991 (the driest since 1921), which, together with global warming, caused the seasons to become drier. All the signs were that we were over-draining the Fens with the seasons becoming drier, but mother nature proved she was in charge and the experts were wrong. My father's words come to mind, relating to the year 1921, when only 12½ inches of rain fell. During that summer the grass died and branches were cut off trees to feed to the cattle to keep them alive. Did they say then that the Fens were over-drained, for if they did they would be proved wrong with 1922 having 26.3 inches and 1927 almost 30 inches in the year.

A modern onion processing plant on the outskirts of Chatteris. (RS)

This wind turbine near Ramsey could be the first of many to come to the Fens. It reminds us of the hundreds of wind engines that adorned this flat landscape in the eighteenth century. (RS)

Many of the Fens' main pumping stations at the outfalls were installed during the 1930s and '40s, and although they have served us well they will need to be upgraded in the near future if the Fens are to be kept as we know them. The amounts of rainfall per month or year are not significantly different today from past levels, but surface run-off has increased, much to the engineers' chagrin. This is due to several factors, but especially urbanisation, particularly on the upper reaches of the rivers where building has been carried out on the flood plains. Urbanisation, together with improved agricultural drainage and soil management, have caused water to pass through the soils into the drains more quickly. A large area of grassland bordering the Fens has been turned over to arable farming, thereby increasing the run-off into many IDB areas. Some IDBs are discovering that small areas on the edge of the Fens are now frequently flooding, which they put down to grassland being turned into arable farming.

He is a brave person who says the Fens are 'over-drained'. This could perhaps be said of some seasons, although this could be put right by better water conservation – if anyone were prepared to fund such an idea. Some farmers and many fen dwellers would welcome the idea, as would the Fenland Waterways Tourism Regeneration Project, as it could change the whole fenland ecosystem and some of

Even though Cowbit Wash has not flooded since the 1950s, many swans still come to feed, but not to breed, in their ancient ancestral home. (RS)

its landscape. It is, however, unlikely to be effected at a time when cheap food is available from around the world and it is debated whether we need an agricultural industry at all. Even more importantly, the scheme would have to cope with freak weather patterns that may occur in the future, patterns we cannot predict but which we know happened in the past.

To the outsider the administration of drainage in the Fens may seem outdated and even medieval. The system works remarkably well, however, much better than many areas in the UK because all the personnel involved, from management to machine operator, know and understand their subject, much of their knowledge handed down from generation to generation from families that live so close to nature. These drainage authorities are run by competent and knowledgeable staff, who are dedicated to their work and respected by farmers and the communities they live with. They are backed up by an elected chairman and board members from the local communities who carry out this work as unpaid representatives.

But the tide of change may sweep again over fen history, and drainage matters will be decided by fewer people, turning the clock back one thousand years, to when a few great abbots and Norman families oversaw the drainage of this land. Over past centuries there have been visionaries who have dreamed of changing the Fens in many ways, some achieving their goal, others not. Some have wanted to change the Fens into a fertile plain, others to the wetland it once was. But because they have been man-made, they will always remain an exciting area to many people, to farm in, to live in, to drain and to flood. It is a part of England that has been created and won for England, and can be lost for England. The greatest danger in front of us today is complacency and to fall into the trap so many of our ancestors fell into, in thinking 'the Fens are now drained'.

The fenman's adversary has not changed over the centuries: he is challenged on three sides, from the sea, from the high country and by the Fens themselves. Nature's challenge to claim back the prize she lost thousands of years ago will go on relentlessly, as long as mankind has the will to continue the battle. It is a never-ending task to ensure we can farm our precious soils and sleep safely in our beds at night. The systems we have today have evolved through the ingenuity of engineers and much local knowledge – history is a great reminder of what could happen in the future. The Danger Bell at Crowland Abbey has tolled twice in the last 120 years, in 1880 and 1947. At Easter-time in 1998 the River Welland was tested to its limit, as was the question of whether the siphons in the Crowland and Cowbit Washes would work. I have my doubts, but as sure as water runs downhill they will be tested one day. I was seven years old when the bell last tolled: will I hear it one more time before I join the burial ground of my ancestors? I hope not, but one day it will toll again to remind us that 'the Fens will never be drained'.

Mrs Horley grading and packing cock pheasant tail feathers at H. Friend, felmongers of Wisbech, in 1954. The Fens is one of the few areas in the country where wild pheasants breed prolifically, thanks to the abundance of reed beds. The feathers are exported worldwide. (LRC)

Acknowledgements

Writing on a subject such as the Fens and endeavouring to cover a period of a thousand years has brought me in contact with many people who are involved in drainage as well as families whose ancestors helped create this unique land. They, together with local historians, fen characters and local people who share my passion for this area, have helped me write this book. Christine Hanson of Bookmark, Spalding, inspired and guided me, as did author Stuart Gibbard. John Honnor shared with me his vast knowledge of the Fens and its drainage, and gave invaluable assistance in providing illustrations, as did Chris Jakes, Christina Swaine of the Lilian Ream Collection *(LRC)*, John Elms and Katie Reddin. Further photographs and illustrations are from the Cambridge Collection *(CC)*, *Harvest Home*, the author's collection *(RS)* or have been kindly loaned by family or friends. Moulding my work into a book would not have been possible without the expert guidance of the staff at Sutton Publishing, in particular Simon Fletcher, Paul Field, Michelle Tilling and Elizabeth Stone. But above all I am indebted to my wife Steph, whose tolerance, encouragement and unending patience has in large measure made possible the publication of this, my first book.

BIBLIOGRAPHY

H.C. Darby, *The Medieval Fenland* (Cambridge University Press, 1940)
William Dugdale, *History of Embanking and Draining* (1772)
Charles Kingsley, *Hereward the Wake* (James Nisbet & Co., n.d.)
S.H. Miller and S.B.J. Skertchly, *The Fenland Past and Present* (1878)
Dorothy Summers, *The Great Level* (David & Charles, 1976)
W.H. Wheeler, *The History of the Fens of South Lincolnshire* (1st edn 1868; repr. Paul Watkins, 1990)